The Spirit of Sacagawea

A Textile Tribute to an American Heroine

＊ LAURIE SIMPSON *and* POLLY MINICK ＊

KANSAS CITY STAR
QUILTS
Continuing the Tradition

The Spirit of Sacagawea
A Textile Tribute to an American Heroine
By Laurie Simpson and Polly Minick

Editor: Edie McGinnis
Book Designer: Amy Robertson
Photography: Aaron T. Leimkuehler
Illustration: Eric Sears
Technical Editor: Jane Miller
Production Assistance: Jo Ann Groves

Published by:
Kansas City Star Books
1729 Grand Blvd.
Kansas City, Missouri, USA 64108

First edition, first printing
ISBN: 978-1-61169-059-0

Library of Congress Control Number: 2012942880

Printed in the United States of America
by Walsworth Publishing Co., Marceline, MO

To order copies, call StarInfo at (816) 234-4636
and say "Books."

Contents

About the Authors.......................2
Acknowledgements......................3
Introduction 4

THE SPIRIT OF SACAGAWEA
Supply list, main quilt...................6
Supply list, alternate version 7

BLOCKS
Bird and Nest.............................8
Mariner's Compass 12
Shining Star................................16
Baby Baskets 20
Crossed Canoes 24
Rocky Mountain Pass 28
Horses 32
Deer Fern..................................36
Chokecherry 40
Salmonberry 44
Log Cabin 48
Stack of Coins............................52
Templates.............................81-102

PROJECTS
Housewife Needle Case 60
Running Horse Needle Punch......66
Salmonberries Penny Rug.............70
Scrap Rug.................................74
Antique Basket of Flowers Rug 78

Laurie Simpson, left,
and Polly Minick, right.

About the Authors

LAURIE SIMPSON

A lifelong needle artist, Laurie's quilts grace galleries and private collections. She has been featured in *Country Home, Coastal Living, Architectural Digest, American Patchwork & Quilting, McCall's Quilting, Quilt Sampler Magazine* and *Quiltmania*.

A patchwork quilt in a magazine inspired Laurie to take up quilting at the age of fourteen. Drawn to traditional themes and techniques, she prefers to piece, appliqué, and quilt by hand. "Handwork is calming and meditative. It's the way I was meant to work," says Laurie.

She joyfully spends her time quilting, creating, teaching, writing and designing fabric for Moda Fabrics with her sister and design partner, Polly Minick.

Laurie lives with her husband, Bill, in Ann Arbor, Michigan. They share their home with Gibby, a rescued Boxer.

POLLY MINICK

Polly Minick began hooking rugs in the '70s. Being an avid antique collector, she wanted a couple of rugs to go with her collections. The rugs she saw at antique shows were not always in great condition, so she decided to make her own.

Her style is primitive and she draws her inspiration from what is around her — family, home, country and nature. Her patriotic works were inspired when her youngest son, Jim, was commissioned an officer in the United States Marine Corps; he is currently serving as a colonel and recently returned from the Middle East. Jim's service has also inspired her to work diligently for Semper Fi, Injured Marine Fund which she says is "a labor of love."

Polly's enthusiasm for fiber art has led her to national acclaim as a creator of primitive-style rugs and is a highly touted guest lecturer. She enjoys traveling the country and meeting with others who share her passion.

Polly and her husband, Tom, currently live in Naples, Florida, with Annie their Airedale to keep them company. They have three grown sons and seven cherished grandchildren who love to visit.

Acknowledgements

I loved creating this book and the quilt that honors the memory of Sacagawea. I could have never done it without the help of my friends.

Leigh Ann Prange who helps me whenever and with whatever project I can think of. Her friendship and sewing expertise is without peer.

Glenn Dragone who will stitch for me at a moments notice. He's a great friend and my quilty kindred spirit.

Debbie "Ducky" Duckworth who does our wool stitchery. She always fits us in, despite her demanding job.

Logan O'Bier who is a constant source of inspiration.

Polly Minick, my sister, who is filled with boundless energy and creativity: a perfect design partner, the Yin to my Yang.

Everyone at Moda Fabrics who encourage and support Polly and I.

Edie McGinnis, Doug Weaver, Diane McLendon at The Kansas City Star for their belief and unflagging support. Amy Robertson, my book designer, who made this book look so beautiful. Eric Sears, the talented artist, who did the illustrations and templates. Aaron Leimkuehler, the photographer who shoots such lovely photographs. Jo Ann Groves, the photo imager who makes sure the color is perfect.

My husband, Bill, who does more than his share so I can obsess about quilts. I am blessed to journey through life with him.

—Laurie Simpson

Introduction

Think of it! An opportunity to chart and map out a navigable, transcontinental route from the Midwest to the Pacific Ocean across the new Louisiana Purchase and it was offered to Meriwether Lewis and William Clark.

Commissioned in 1804 by President Thomas Jefferson, the "Corps of Discovery" was launched. Up until that time, only a few people — Native Americans and fur traders — were known to travel from Missouri to the Pacific Ocean and back. Jefferson knew if the country were to grow and thrive, it must move ever westward and an accurate route must be mapped.

After months of planning, the Corps of Discovery led by Lewis and Clark departed on May 14th, 1804. Thirty-three participants left the Illinois Territory to begin their journey. In Lewis's own words, they were "good hunters, stout healthy unmarried young men, accustomed to the woods and capable of bearing bodily fatigue to a pretty considerable degree."

At Fort Mandan, one of their early stops near present day Washburn, North Dakota, they met a French-Canadian fur trader named Toussaint Charbonneau. Charbonneau was added to the Corps as an experienced trader, Indian guide and translator.

Charbonneau had overstated his proficiency in both his navigation and translation skills. Although he gave her

Left: Sacagawea monument in Portland, Oregon. Inset: A map by Lewis and Clark. All images courtesy the Library of Congress.

little credit, his language skills were mostly due to his young Shoshone bride — Sacagawea.

Sacagawea had been kidnapped by the Mandans in her youth. Even though she had been taken from the Shoshones as a young girl, she remembered landmarks and villages. She must have looked forward to seeing her family again.

Like most Native Americans, she had been taught about fruits, berries, edible plants, and hunting as a young girl. Her knowledge was one more asset the Corp would come to value.

She was resourceful and brave; she fearlessly swam and rescued much needed supplies after their dug out canoes overturned, and she gave birth early in the journey and traveled with the infant. This alone should endear her to every woman who reads of her life.

The Corps of Discovery was also charged with the task of chronicling the flora and fauna they discovered on the journey. Lewis and Clark's journals did more than document their travels and route across the Northwest. They also told of their day-to-day ordeals and struggles. Drawings of birds and plants were sketched onto some of the pages. And they recorded their encounters with the Native Americans they met.

Little did Lewis and Clark know that of all the people traveling in their party, a young woman would stand out above all others.

Sacagawea was a real person — a woman, a young mother, a strong, brave, headstrong pioneer.

I am honored to tell her story in thread and cloth.

The Spirit of Sacagawea

Designed and stitched
by Laurie Simpson.
Quilt Size: 66" x 84" Finished

SUPPLY LIST

* 4¾ yards of background fabric
* 4½ yards total of assorted red fabrics —
  reserve ¾ yard for binding.
* 2¼ yards total of assorted blue fabrics
* ½ yard total of assorted tan fabrics
* Scraps of black fabric
  (enough to equal a 12" square)
* Scraps of gold fabric
  (enough to equal a 10" square)
* Blue embroidery floss
* ¼" bias tape maker
* ⅜" bias tape maker
* ½" bias tape maker
* 1" circle paper punch – optional

6

Alternate Version

Designed by Laurie Simpson, made by
Leigh Ann Prange, quilted by Kari Ruedisale.
Quilt Size: 72" x 94½" Finished.

SUPPLY LIST

❋ 3¾ yards total light backgrounds:
❋ 3¾ yards total assorted med. neutral
  fabrics – reserve 1½ yards of one of the
  neutrals for the sashing
❋ 2¼ yards total assorted red fabrics
❋ 4½ yards total assorted black/grays/
  darks – reserve 2¾ yards of one of the
  darks for sashing and binding

❋ ½ yard assorted purples
❋ 1 fat quarter assorted gold scraps
❋ Assorted dark neutral embroidery floss –
  enough to amount to one skein
❋ ¼" bias tape maker
❋ ⅜" bias tape maker
❋ ½" bias tape maker
❋ 1" circle paper punch – optional

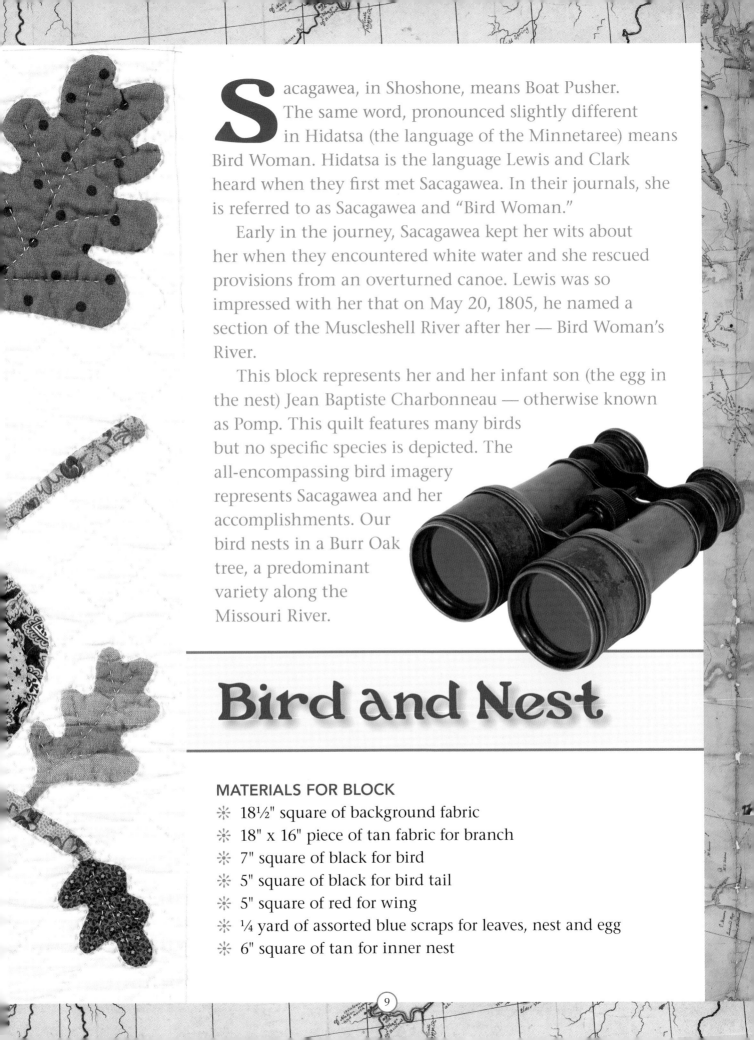

S acagawea, in Shoshone, means Boat Pusher. The same word, pronounced slightly different in Hidatsa (the language of the Minnetaree) means Bird Woman. Hidatsa is the language Lewis and Clark heard when they first met Sacagawea. In their journals, she is referred to as Sacagawea and "Bird Woman."

Early in the journey, Sacagawea kept her wits about her when they encountered white water and she rescued provisions from an overturned canoe. Lewis was so impressed with her that on May 20, 1805, he named a section of the Muscleshell River after her — Bird Woman's River.

This block represents her and her infant son (the egg in the nest) Jean Baptiste Charbonneau — otherwise known as Pomp. This quilt features many birds but no specific species is depicted. The all-encompassing bird imagery represents Sacagawea and her accomplishments. Our bird nests in a Burr Oak tree, a predominant variety along the Missouri River.

Bird and Nest

MATERIALS FOR BLOCK

* 18½" square of background fabric
* 18" x 16" piece of tan fabric for branch
* 7" square of black for bird
* 5" square of black for bird tail
* 5" square of red for wing
* ¼ yard of assorted blue scraps for leaves, nest and egg
* 6" square of tan for inner nest

Bird and Nest

BLOCK ASSEMBLY INSTRUCTIONS

You will find the templates for this block on pages 82 – 85.

1. Fold the background fabric in half vertically and horizontally. Finger press the creases in place and open.

2. Cut out the appliqué elements, adding ⅛" – ¼" seam allowance.

3. Appliqué the shapes in place in the following order: branch (leaving openings where the leaves will go), leaves, outer nest, inner nest, egg, bird body, bird tail and bird wing.

4. Press.

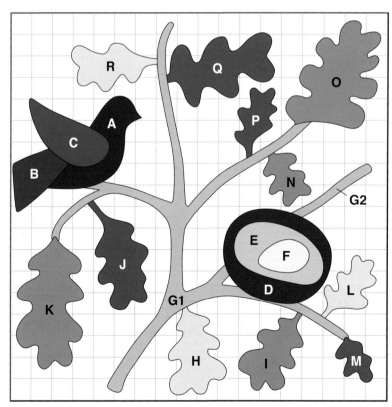

1 Square = 1"

Bird and Nest Alternate Version

MATERIALS FOR BLOCK

❉ 18½" square of background fabric

❉ 18" x 16" dark neutral for branch

❉ Assorted dark neutrals for bird and bird tail – enough to equal an 8" square

❉ Assorted purples for leaves – enough to equal an 8" square

❉ Assorted reds for bird wing and leaves – enough to equal a 10" square

❉ Assorted medium neutrals for leaves and nest – enough to equal ⅛ yard

❉ Assorted lights for inside nest and egg – enough to equal a 9" square

❉ 9" square of gold for leaves

BLOCK ASSEMBLY INSTRUCTIONS

Follow the directions given to make the block. Refer to the above photo for color placement.

The Mariner's Compass block represents Sacagawea's role as a guide during the Corp of Discovery. Her role didn't start out that way. Lewis and Clark hired her husband, Toussaint Charbonneau as a guide and translator, yet Charbonneau had never been as far west as the expedition was planning to go and did not speak Shoshone. Charbonneau, while not well equipped, knew his wife capable of both. Once westward and out of familiar territory, they relied more and more on Sacagawea to point out landmarks.

When the Corp did meet up with the Shoshone, Sacagawea would translate to Hidatsu to Charbonneau and he would translate to French. Members of the Corp all knew some French and between them all, they could parse it out.

This classic quilt block represents the arduous journey from Missouri to the Coast of Oregon and back. Surprising everyone, the native girl was more and more an integral part of the expedition.

Mariner's Compass

MATERIALS:
* ½ yard background fabric
* ⅛ yard assorted reds for compass points and center
* 1 fat eighth light blue for compass points
* 10" square medium blue for compass points
* 10" square dark blue for compass points

Mariner's Compass

CUTTING INSTRUCTIONS

From background fabric, cut
* 4 pieces using template F
* 32 pieces using template E taking care to notice the grain line of the template markings.

From red fabric, cut
* 16 pieces using template D
* 1 circle using template G

From light blue fabric, cut
* 8 pieces using template C

From medium blue fabric, cut
* 4 pieces using template A

From dark blue fabric, cut
* 4 pieces using template B

BLOCK ASSEMBLY INSTRUCTIONS

You will find the templates for this block on pages 86 – 87.

1. Sew a background E piece to either side of a red D piece. Make 16. Press the seams to the outside. Refer to the placement diagram if necessary.

2. Sew E/D unit to each side of a light blue C piece. You should have 8 E/D/C units. Press the seams to the outside. Refer to the placement diagram if necessary.

3. Sew an E/D/C unit to either side of a dark blue B piece. You will have 4 E/D/C/B units. Press the seams to the outside. Refer to the placement diagram if necessary.

4. Sew a medium blue A piece to one side of the E/D/C/B units, taking care to sew it on the same side of each unit. Press the seams to the outside. Refer to the placement diagram if necessary.

5. Sew the 4 units together.

6. Sew the short sides of piece F together to make the "frame" for the compass. Press the seams open.

7. Mark the tick marks for each point on the seam allowance of piece F. Match up the compass points with the tick marks, pin and stitch in place.

8. Turn the edges of the red G circle under and appliqué in place over the hole in the center of the block.

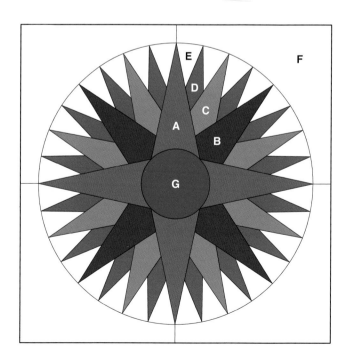

MATERIALS FOR BLOCK
✳ ¼ yard light background for circle
✳ ¼ yard medium neutral for background
✳ Assorted reds for compass points and center – enough to equal ⅛ yard
✳ Assorted dark and medium neutrals for compass points – enough to equal ¼ yard. We used 3 different neutrals.

BLOCK ASSEMBLY INSTRUCTIONS
Follow the directions given to make the block. Refer to the above photo for color placement.

The Corp of Discovery encountered many different tribes of native people on their journey, including Minnetaree, Mandan, Arikara, and Cree. Their first extended stop was at Fort Mandan where they met Charbonneau and Sacagawea. Fort Mandan was populated by several tribes and was situated in what is now North Dakota. Today, the most populous Native American tribe in both North and South Dakota are the Lakota — or Sioux.

Since the 1880s, the Lakota nation has used an 8-pointed star as their tribal symbol and incorporated patchwork as well. Many Lakota people consider an 8-pointed star (or LeMoyne star in quilter language) to be an iconic image of their heritage, as it closely coincides with their traditional symbol — the Morning, or Shining Star. Shining Stars are found on everyday items and clothing in either paint or beadwork. Star quilts are used in many rites of passage of a Lakota; they are given in marriage and often accompany a Lakota into burial. In honor of this custom, we have included the Shining Star into Sacagawea's quilt.

Shining Star

MATERIALS FOR BLOCK
* Fat quarter of background fabric
* 4" x 40" of red fabric
* 8" x 40" of light blue fabric
* 8" x 40" of dark blue fabric

Shining Star

CUTTING INSTRUCTIONS

From the background fabric, cut
* 4 – 5¾" squares or use template A
* 1 – 8¾" square, cut **twice** diagonally or cut 4 using template B

From the red fabric, cut
* 4 – 1¾" x 22" strips

From the light blue fabric, cut
* 8 – 1¾" x 22" strips

From the dark blue fabric, cut
* 6 – 1¾" x 22" strips

BLOCK ASSEMBLY INSTRUCTIONS

You will find the templates for this block on page 88.

1. Sew a red, light blue and dark blue strip set together, offsetting the strips by approximately 2". Make 4. Press the seams to one side.

2. Cut a 45-degree angle off one end of the strip set.

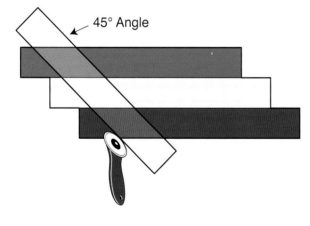

45° Angle

3. Using a ruler, cut 16 slices of these 4 strip sets that are 1¾" wide. Set aside.

4. Sew a light blue, a dark blue, and a light blue strip set together, offsetting the strips approximately 2". Make 2. Press the seams to one side. (See above graphics if necessary.)

5. Cut a 45-degree angle off one end of the strip set.

6. Using a ruler, cut 8 slices off of these 2 strip sets that are 1¾" wide. Set aside.

7. Sew 1 red, light blue, dark blue strip set to either side of a light blue, dark blue, light blue strip set. Repeat for a total of 8. Press the seams to one side.

8. Refer to the diagram and sew 2 diamonds together. Stop and start your seam ¼" away from the edge and trim off the "dog-ears." Repeat for the remaining diamonds.

9. Sew a background A square into each diamond pair. Press the seams to the side.

10. Sew the 4 units together into a star. Press the seams open.

11. Set the 4 background B triangles into the sides of the star. Press the seams to the side.

MATERIALS FOR BLOCK
✳ Fat quarter of light background fabric
✳ 4" x 40" strip of red fabric
✳ 8" x 40" strip of dark neutral fabric
✳ 8" x 40" strip of light neutral fabric

BLOCK ASSEMBLY INSTRUCTIONS
Follow the directions given to make the block. Refer to the above photo for color placement.

S acagawea gave birth to Jean Baptiste Charbonneau, also known as Pomp, in the winter of 1805. Several weeks later she set out with the Corp of Discovery. Pomp spent much of his time in a cradleboard made of willows, strapped to Sacagawea's back. The willow frame of the cradleboard was covered with softened, tanned hide and a willow visor shielded the baby's face. During the cold winter months, it was lined in rabbit fur.

The small 6" individual basket block is listed in Barbara Brackman's *Encyclopedia of Pieced Quilt Patterns* as Baby Bunting. We grouped four Baby Bunting baskets together with a zigzag border to make our Baby Baskets block.

Baby Baskets

MATERIALS FOR BLOCK

❋ ½ yard background fabric

❋ 3" x 12" of 4 different fabrics for baskets

❋ 1 – 5" x 12½" rectangle of fabric for block border center strips (We used a blue stripe.)

❋ ¼ yard red for border

❋ 1 – 4" x 18" strip of fabric for the border corners (We used a blue/red print.)

Baby Baskets

CUTTING INSTRUCTIONS

From the background fabric, cut
* ☀ 12 – 2" squares or use template A
* ☀ 2 – 3⅞" squares cut in half diagonally or 4 triangles using template E
* ☀ 2 – 4¼" squares cut in half diagonally twice or 8 triangles using template C
* ☀ 8 – 2" x 3½" rectangles or use template D
* ☀ 44 – triangles using template F
* ☀ 4 – triangles using template G
* ☀ 4 – triangles using template Gr

From the blue/red print, cut
* ☀ 4 – 3½" squares

From the red fabric, cut
* ☀ 44 border triangles using template F
* ☀ 4 – triangles using template G
* ☀ 4 – triangles using template Gr

From the blue stripe, cut
* ☀ 4 – 1" x 12½" border center strips

From each of the 4 basket fabrics, cut:
* ☀ 2 – 2" squares (template A)
* ☀ 3 – 2⅜" squares cut in half diagonally or 6 triangles using template B

BLOCK ASSEMBLY INSTRUCTIONS

You will find the templates for this block on page 89.

1. Sew a dark 2" A square to a background 2" A square. Make two and sew into a 4-patch unit. Press the seams to the dark.

2. Sew a dark B triangle onto each side of a background C triangle, making a flying geese unit. Make two. Press the seams to one side.

3. Sew a dark B triangle to one end of a background D rectangle. Make 2. Refer to the placement diagram to position the triangles. Press the seams toward the dark fabric.

4. Sew a background A square to one side of a flying geese unit. Press.

5. Sew the other flying geese unit to the center 4-patch. Press the seams to one side.

6. Refer to the placement diagram and sew the small square/flying geese unit to this one. Press.

7. Sew the 2 rectangle/triangle units to the sides of this larger unit. Refer to the placement diagram if necessary.

8. Sew the large background E triangle onto the base of this unit. Press the seam to one side. This will complete one basket. Make 4.

9. Refer to the placement diagram and sew the four baskets together to complete the center of the block.

10. Refer to the diagram and sew 6 red F triangles and 5 background F triangles together.

11. Sew a background G triangle to one end of the strip and a background Gr to the other.

12. Now make a strip by sewing 6 background F triangles and 5 red F triangles together.

13. Sew a red G triangle to one end of the strip and a red Gr to the other. Sew the two strips you have just made onto either side of a blue-striped center 1" strip. Make 4. Press the seams to one side.

14. Sew a border onto each side of the basket block. Press the seams to the outside.

15. Sew a 4" corner square onto each end of the remaining 2 border sections. Press the seams to the outside.

16. Sew one to the top and one to the bottom of your block. Press the seams to the outside.

MATERIALS FOR BLOCK

❊ ½ yard background fabric
❊ Assorted red fabrics for baskets and border – enough to equal ½ yard
❊ Assorted purples for baskets and corner squares – enough to equal 1 fat quarter
❊ 8" square of dark neutral for basket

BLOCK ASSEMBLY INSTRUCTIONS

Follow the directions given to make the block. Refer to the above photo for color placement.

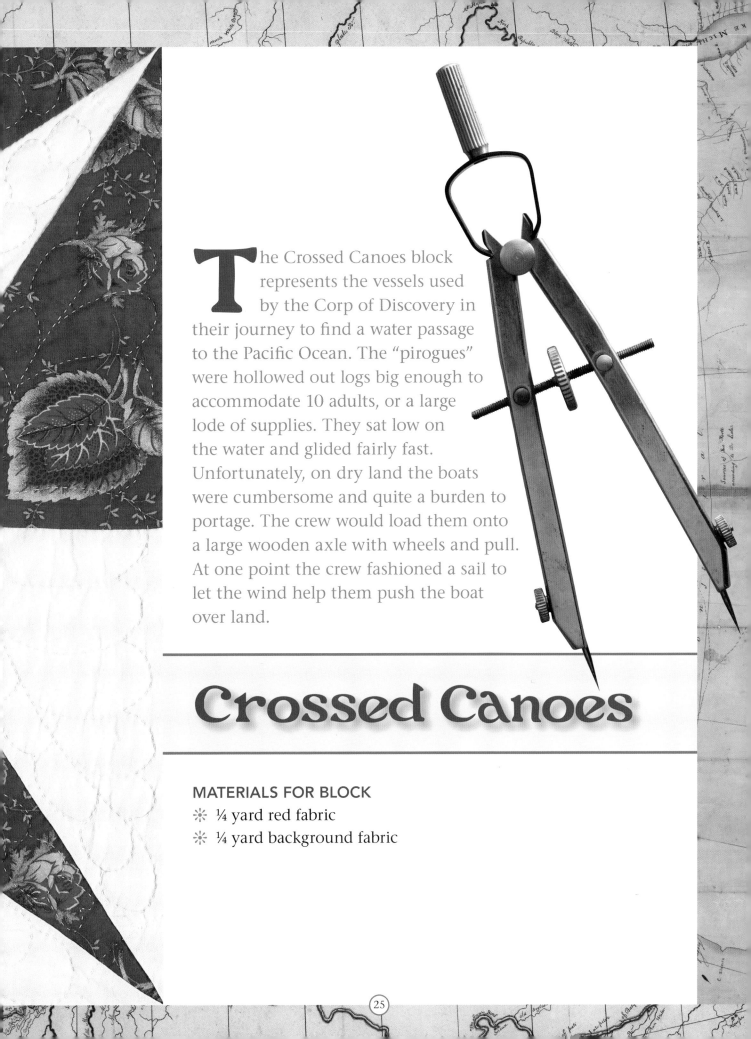

The Crossed Canoes block represents the vessels used by the Corp of Discovery in their journey to find a water passage to the Pacific Ocean. The "pirogues" were hollowed out logs big enough to accommodate 10 adults, or a large lode of supplies. They sat low on the water and glided fairly fast. Unfortunately, on dry land the boats were cumbersome and quite a burden to portage. The crew would load them onto a large wooden axle with wheels and pull. At one point the crew fashioned a sail to let the wind help them push the boat over land.

Crossed Canoes

MATERIALS FOR BLOCK
* ¼ yard red fabric
* ¼ yard background fabric

Crossed Canoes

CUTTING INSTRUCTIONS

From the red fabric, cut
* 2 pieces using template A
* 2 pieces using template Ar
* 2 pieces using template B
* 2 pieces using template C

From the background fabric, cut
* 2 pieces using template A
* 2 pieces using template Ar
* 2 pieces using template B
* 2 pieces using template C

BLOCK ASSEMBLY INSTRUCTIONS

You will find the templates for this block on pages 90 – 91.

1. Sew a background A and Ar to either side of a red B triangle. Add a background C triangle. Make 2. Press the seams to the outside.

2. Sew a red A and Ar to a background B triangle. Add a red C triangle. Press the seams to the outside. Make two.

3. Refer to the placement diagram and sew these 4 sections together. Press the seams toward the dark fabric.

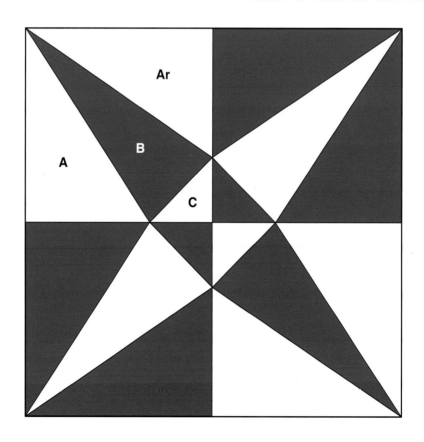

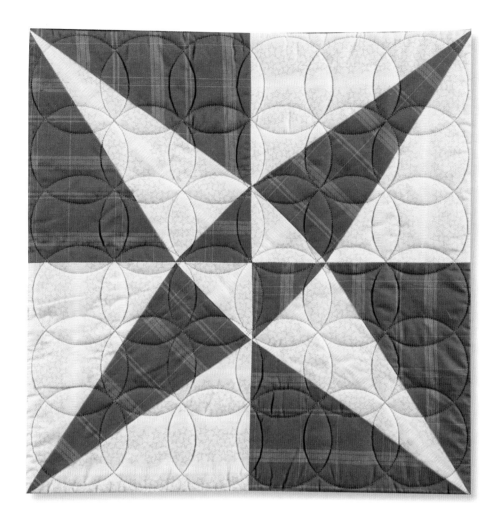

MATERIALS FOR BLOCK
- ✳ ¼ yard light background
- ✳ ¼ yard red

BLOCK ASSEMBLY INSTRUCTIONS
Follow the directions given to make the block. Refer to the above photo for color placement.

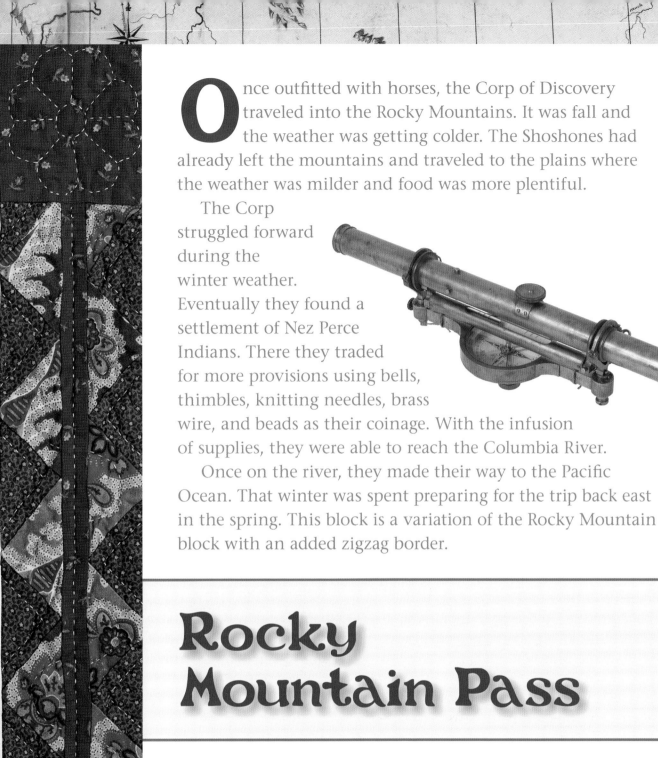

O nce outfitted with horses, the Corp of Discovery traveled into the Rocky Mountains. It was fall and the weather was getting colder. The Shoshones had already left the mountains and traveled to the plains where the weather was milder and food was more plentiful.

The Corp struggled forward during the winter weather. Eventually they found a settlement of Nez Perce Indians. There they traded for more provisions using bells, thimbles, knitting needles, brass wire, and beads as their coinage. With the infusion of supplies, they were able to reach the Columbia River.

Once on the river, they made their way to the Pacific Ocean. That winter was spent preparing for the trip back east in the spring. This block is a variation of the Rocky Mountain block with an added zigzag border.

Rocky Mountain Pass

MATERIALS FOR BLOCK

❋ 1 – 13½" square of background fabric
❋ 1 – 8" square of gold fabric
❋ 12" total of assorted scraps of red fabric for sun
❋ 1 – 12½" square of red for border
❋ ¼ yard dark blue for border
❋ ¼ yard medium blue for border

Rocky Mountain Pass

CUTTING INSTRUCTIONS

From the background fabric, cut
* 1 piece using template F
* 6 pieces using template C
* 2 pieces using template E
* 2 pieces using template Er

From the gold fabric, cut
* 2 pieces using template A

From the medium blue fabric, cut
* 36 pieces using template G
* 8 triangles using template H

From the red fabric, cut
* 2 pieces using template B
* 8 pieces using template D
* 4 – 1" x 12½" strips (No template given)
* 4 – 3½" squares. (No template given)

From the dark blue fabric, cut
* 36 pieces using template G
* 8 triangles using template H

BLOCK ASSEMBLY INSTRUCTIONS

You will find the templates for this block on pages 92 – 93.

1. Sew the gold piece A to the red piece B. Press the seams to the outside.

2. Sew 4 red D pieces to 3 background C pieces. End the curved D/C strip with a background E piece on 1 end and a background Er piece on the other. Press the seams to one side.

3. Sew this to the A/B section. Make 2 of the sun sections. Press the seams to the outside.

4. Sew the two sun sections to piece F. Press the seams to the outside.

5. Refer to the diagram and sew 5 dark blue G triangles and 4 medium blue G triangles together. End the strip with a medium blue H triangle. Then sew 5 medium blue H triangles to 4 dark blue triangles. End the strip with a dark H triangle on either end of the strip. Refer to the diagram and sew the strips to either side of the red 1" x 12½" strip. Make 4. Press the seams to one side.

6. Sew a border onto each side of the Rocky Mountain block.

7. Sew a red 3½" corner square onto each end of the remaining 2 border sections. Press the seams to the outside.

8. Sew one border to the top and the other to the bottom of the block.

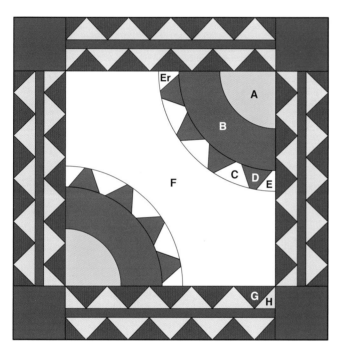

MATERIALS FOR BLOCK

* 13" square of light background fabric
* 8" square of gold fabric
* Assorted dark neutral fabrics for sun and border – enough to equal ½ yard
* 12" square of purple for suns
* 12 ½" square of red for border corners and border sashing

BLOCK ASSEMBLY INSTRUCTIONS

Follow the directions given to make the block. Refer to the above photo for color placement.

"The Shoshones are a small tribe of the nation called the Snake Indians, a vague appellation, which embraces at once the inhabitants of the southern parts of the Rocky Mountains and of the plains on either side."

—*First Across The Continents: The Story of The Exploring Expedition of Lewis and Clark in 1804-05-06* by Noah Brooks

L ewis and Clark knew that if their endeavor was to be a success, they would eventually need to trade for horses to cross the continental divide en route to the Pacific. The people in the Rocky Mountains – the Shoshones were known to have great horses. Because Sacagawea was of Shoshone birth, she acted as the go-between in this transaction. This was particularly serendipitous since the Tribal Chief they would be trading with was Sacagawea's brother, Cameahwait. After receiving the horses from the Shoshone, Lewis and Clark promised goods from the west when they returned from the Pacific.

Horses

MATERIALS FOR BLOCK
* 1 – 18½" background square
* 2 – 10" x 17" red rectangles

Horses

BLOCK ASSEMBLY INSTRUCTIONS

You will find the templates for this block on pages 93 – 94.

1. Fold the background fabric in half horizontally and vertically and finger press.

2. Cut 1 and 1 reversed horse from the red fabric, using template A. Be sure you add ⅛" – ¼" seam allowance when cutting around the template.

3. Appliqué the horses onto the background block.

1 Square = 1"

MATERIALS FOR BLOCK

❋ 18½" square of light background fabric
❋ 2 – 10" x 17" dark neutral rectangles

BLOCK ASSEMBLY INSTRUCTIONS

Follow the directions given to make the block. Refer to the above photo for color placement.

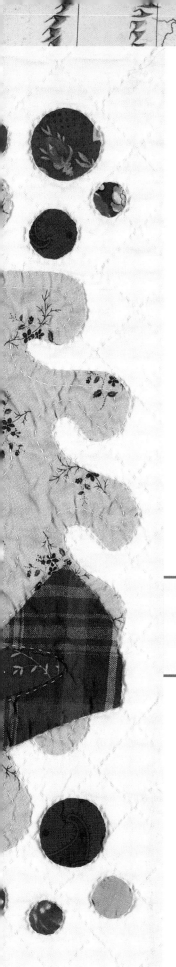

The Deer Fern was one of the plants documented in the journals of Lewis and Clark. It was their intent to record as much flora, fauna and natural resources as possible on their journey. For many of the species they wrote about, it was the first time they were documented in print.

Deer Fern is found mostly in the Pacific Northwest and in the spring it's one of the first green shoots to appear. This quilt block has a resting bird on a wreath of lobed fern fronds, and the currants represent golden currants found in the Cascade Mountains.

Deer Fern

MATERIALS FOR BLOCK

❋ 1 – 18½" square of background fabric
❋ 1 – 18½" square of light blue fabric
❋ 10" total assorted red scraps
❋ 3" total assorted gold scraps

Deer Fern

BLOCK ASSEMBLY INSTRUCTIONS

You will find the templates for this block on pages 96 – 97.

1. Fold the background fabric in half vertically and horizontally. Finger press the creases for placement purposes.

2. Refer to the templates and cut out the necessary appliqué elements, adding ⅛" – ¼" seam allowance.

3. Appliqué the pieces onto the background in the following order: wreath, bird beak, bird body, wing and currants.

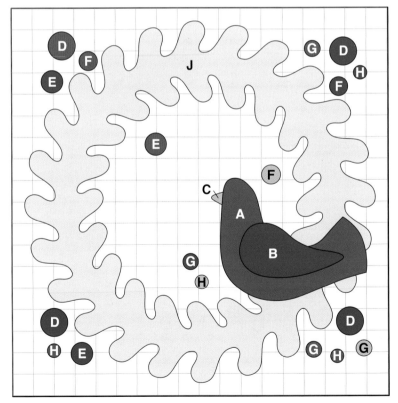

1 Square = 1"

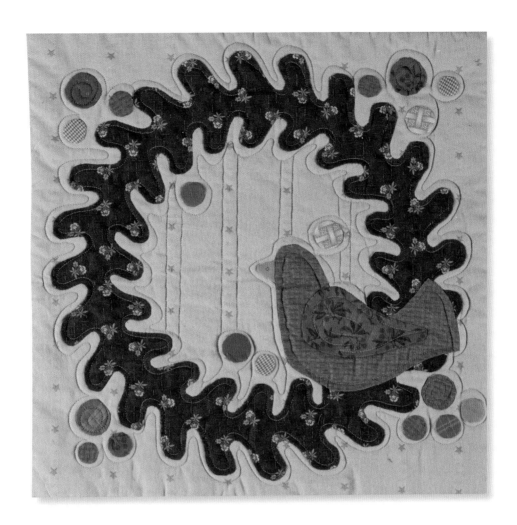

MATERIALS FOR BLOCK
✳ 18½" square of light background fabric
✳ 18½" square of purple fabric for wreath
✳ Assorted red fabrics – enough to equal a 10" square
✳ 3" square of gold fabric

BLOCK ASSEMBLY INSTRUCTIONS
Follow the directions given to make the block. Refer to the above photo for color placement.

Chokecherries were found in the Pacific Northwest and were particularly abundant in the Cascade Mountains. Native Americans collected the fruit in the fall, pounded them flat, often leaving the stones in place, and dried them. The wood of the chokecherry tree was used for basket handles and shredded bark for basket rims. Native women also made a tonic from the bark and drank it after childbirth to restore their strength. Wildlife also fed off the fruit. Birds, black bears and raccoons feasted on the fruit while chipmunks and deer mice carried off only the stones. Our chokecherry quilt block shows cheerful birds feeding from Nature's bounty.

Chokecherry

MATERIALS FOR BLOCK

* 1 – 18½" square of background fabric
* 1 – fat quarter (18" x 22") total of assorted blue fabric
* 1 – 12" square total of assorted red fabrics
* 1 – 4" x 7" scrap of tan fabric
* Blue embroidery floss
* ⅜" bias tape maker
* 1" circle paper punch – optional

Chokecherry

CUTTING INSTRUCTIONS

From the assorted blue fabrics, cut
- ❋ 2 – ¾" x 26" bias strips (cut on the diagonal of a fat quarter) and save the rest for appliqué
- ❋ 20 leaves using template D
- ❋ 1 bird using template E

From the tan fabric, cut
- ❋ One vase using template A

From the assorted red fabrics, cut
- ❋ One bird using template B
- ❋ 23 – 1½" circles for the cherries. (I used a 1" circle paper punch from a scrapbooking store to make my templates.) Punch out 23 circles from card stock or cut using template C. Place a 1" card circle in the center of the fabric circle. Run a basting stitch around the edge of the fabric circle and pull tightly. Knot off the thread and clip. Spray with spray starch and press until dry. Cool and take out the paper circle and the fabric circle will snap back into shape.

BLOCK ASSEMBLY

You will find the templates for this block on pages 98.

1. Make the vines using a ⅜" bias maker and the ¾" bias strips.

2. Appliqué the pieces to the background fabric in the following order: vine (bias first, then embroidered stems using 2 strands of embroidery floss and a stem stitch), leaves, cherries, birds and vase.

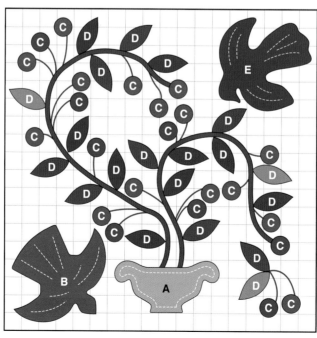

1 Square = 1"

MATERIALS FOR BLOCK

✳ 18½" square background fabric – we used a medium neutral

✳ Assorted dark neutral fabrics for vines, leaves, bird – enough to equal 1 fat quarter

✳ Assorted reds for bird, berries and leaves – enough to equal a 12" square

✳ Assorted medium neutrals for leaves – enough to equal a 6" square

✳ 8" square of purple for vase

✳ Dark neutral embroidery floss

BLOCK ASSEMBLY INSTRUCTIONS

Follow the directions given to make the block. Refer to the above photo for color placement.

The salmonberry is indigenous to the Pacific Northwest. It is much like a raspberry but has orange or salmon-colored fruit at maturity, and is a close cousin to the thimbleberry. Salmonberries are a treat for both people and wildlife.

Native Americans ate not only the fruit but also the tender spring shoots. They made a tea from the leaves and used it as a cure for dysentery. The plant was one of the species documented by Lewis and Clark in their journals.

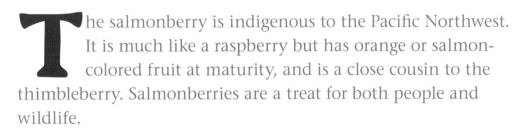

Our Salmonberry block is a folksy tribute to native flora and woven baskets.

Salmonberry

MATERIALS FOR BLOCK

- 1 – 18½" square of background fabric
- 18" x 22" total of assorted blue fabrics
- 18" x 22" total of assorted red fabrics
- ½" bias tape maker
- ¼" bias tape maker

Salmonberry

CUTTING INSTRUCTIONS

Refer to the templates for cutting directions. Add ⅛" – ¼" for seam allowances when cutting out the appliqué elements.

BLOCK ASSEMBLY INSTRUCTIONS

You will find the templates for this block on page 100.

1. Fold the background fabric in half vertically and horizontally and finger press.

2. Cut ⅝" bias strips from blue fabric and use the ¼" bias tape maker to make the vines. (The extra ⅛" in this small cut helps with the accuracy.)

3. Stitch the vines onto the block with the exception of the vine that drapes over the basket. We'll do that one later.

4. Cut 1" bias strips. Make the ribs of the basket using the ½" bias tape maker.

5. Sew the ribs in place and add the center basket rib last to cover the raw edges of the basket pieces.

6. Next, appliqué the basket base and basket rim. (Leave a spot unsewn for the last vine.)

7. Sew on the leaf that is on the right side of the basket, add the last vine, then finish appliquéing the basket rim.

8. Appliqué the rest of the pieces to the block in the following order: leaves, berries, berry caps and bird.

1 Square = 1"

MATERIALS FOR BLOCK

❋ 18½" square of light background fabric
❋ Assorted red fabrics for vase and berries – enough to equal 1 fat quarter
❋ Assorted medium and dark neutrals for leaves, vines, and berry caps – enough to equal 1 fat quarter
❋ 6" square of purple for bird

BLOCK ASSEMBLY INSTRUCTIONS

Follow the directions given to make the block. Refer to the above photo for color placement.

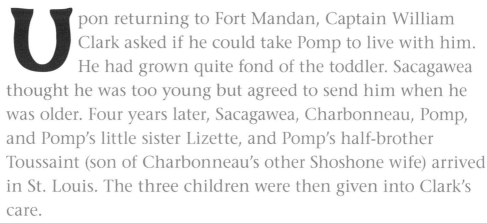

Upon returning to Fort Mandan, Captain William Clark asked if he could take Pomp to live with him. He had grown quite fond of the toddler. Sacagawea thought he was too young but agreed to send him when he was older. Four years later, Sacagawea, Charbonneau, Pomp, and Pomp's little sister Lizette, and Pomp's half-brother Toussaint (son of Charbonneau's other Shoshone wife) arrived in St. Louis. The three children were then given into Clark's care.

It was not uncommon for a family member or friend with means to take in children who lived far from schools. It was often the only way parents could provide a formal education for their children.

Pomp was 18 and working at a trading post on the Kansas River when he met the German Prince Paul Wilhelm of Wurttemberg. Pomp accompanied the prince to Europe where he lived for six years before returning to the west as a guide, trapper and gold miner.

The log cabin block represents the end of the expedition for the Corp of Discovery. We have included Seaman, the large black Newfoundland dog, who was a constant companion for the Corp during their travels.

Log Cabin

MATERIALS FOR BLOCK
* 1 – 18½" square of background fabric
* 10" total assorted dark blue fabric
* 1 – 6" square medium blue fabric
* 1 – 6" square light blue fabric
* 1 – 4" square navy with star fabric for flag canton
* 14" total assorted tan fabrics
* 14" total assorted red fabrics
* 1 – 7" square red striped fabric for flag
* Blue embroidery floss

Log Cabin

CUTTING INSTRUCTIONS

From tan fabric, cut

❇ 1 – 8" x 3" rectangle (this will be used for the "chinking" that goes behind the cabin logs)

❇ Refer to the templates for cutting instructions. Be sure to add ⅛" – ¼" seam allowance when cutting out the pieces.

BLOCK ASSEMBLY INSTRUCTIONS

You will find the templates for this block on pages 101 – 102.

1. Fold the background fabric in half horizontally and vertically and finger press.

2. Embroider the cherry stems using 2 strands of embroidery floss and a stem stitch.

3. Appliqué the cabin "chinking" in place first. Sew the two sides in place, but leave the top and bottom edges free.

4. Appliqué the rest of the pieces in the following order: light blue roof, dark blue roof, logs, door, chimney, bird, dog, cherry leaves, cherries (made like the cherries in the previous block), stripes of the flag, flag canton, flag pole.

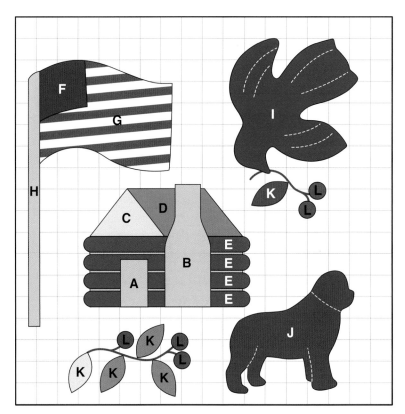

1 Square = 1"

MATERIALS FOR BLOCK

❋ 18½" square of light background fabric

❋ Assorted dark neutrals for flag pole, flag canton, dog, chimney, chinking, roof, door and leaves – enough to equal 1 fat quarter

❋ Assorted medium neutrals for logs and leaves – enough to equal a 14" square

❋ Assorted reds for bird, flag, and berries – enough to equal a 14" square

❋ Neutral embroidery floss

BLOCK ASSEMBLY INSTRUCTIONS

Follow the directions given to make the block. Refer to the above photo for color placement.

No one could have known the importance of Sacagawea's inclusion in the Corp of Discovery. At first, she was just the wife of the guide with the possibility of being able to help with translation. She proved to be so much more! All of the Corp was impressed with her courage and fortitude. She kept a level head when the boats capsized in white water. Her familiarity with the landscape and Hidatsu and Shoshone languages was vital to the success of the mission.

Once they reached the Pacific, the Corp needed to set up camp for the remaining winter of 1806 to prepare for the return trip. In making their decision where to decamp, all were asked their opinion — Sacagawea included. Some scholars believe this was the first recorded democratic vote on American soil that included a woman's vote.

Sacagawea's legacy has been memorialized by The United States mint by striking a coin in her honor using the images of her and her son Pomp. The one-dollar coin was first produced in 2000. It has been struck every year since and will continue to be minted until at least 2016. The Stack of Coins block is representative of this honor.

Stack of Coins

MATERIALS FOR BLOCK
✳ 18½" x 4" strip of background fabric
✳ ⅓ yard total of red, blue and tan scraps

Stack of Coins

CUTTING INSTRUCTIONS

From the background fabric, cut
❋ 2 – 18½" x 2" strips

From assorted scraps, cut
❋ 36 – 5½" x 2" rectangles

BLOCK ASSEMBLY INSTRUCTIONS

1. Sew 12 rectangles "coins" together in a vertical strip. Make three. Press the seams to one side.

2. Sew the 2 background strips to the 3 coin strips. Press the seams to one side.

1 ½" x 5"
finished

1 ½" x 18"
finished

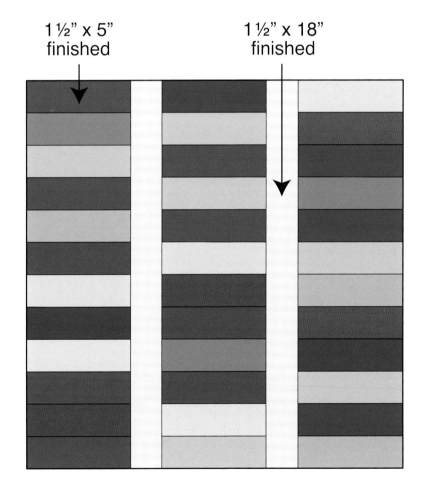

MATERIALS FOR BLOCK

❋ 18½" x 4" strip of light background fabric

❋ Assorted red, purple, medium neutral and dark neutral scraps – enough to equal ⅓ yard

BLOCK ASSEMBLY INSTRUCTIONS

Follow the directions given to make the block. Refer to the above photo for color placement.

Finishing Main Quilt

Refer to the diagram and sew the blocks together into 4 rows of 3 blocks each. Add borders, layer with batting and backing and quilt. Make 2¼" bias binding and sew in place.

BORDERS
MATERIALS
❋ 1 yard background fabric
❋ 1¼ yards assorted red fabrics

CUTTING INSTRUCTIONS
From the background fabric, cut
❋ 6 – 6⅛" x 40" strips. Using template A, cut 80 light triangles and 4 B and 4 Br half-triangles

From the assorted red fabrics, cut
❋ 6 – 6⅛" x 40" strips. Using template A, cut 84 red triangles
❋ 4 – 6⅛" squares for cornerstones

Note: While we have provided templates for the border pieces, there are rulers on the market such as the Simpli-EZ 30 degree Triangle by Darlene Zimmerman that makes constructing this type of border seem like child's play. Not only does it make cutting easier, it does much of the math for you.

BORDER ASSEMBLY
You will find the templates for the borders on page 85.

1. Sew 24 red A triangles and 23 background A triangles together. Finish the row with a background B triangle on one end and a background Br triangle on the remaining end. Make 2. Press the seams to one side. Sew these borders on to the left and right sides of your quilt top, making sure to orient the points correctly.

2. Sew 18 red A triangles to 17 light A triangles together. End the row with a background B triangle on one end and a background Br triangle on the remaining end. Make two. Press the seams to one side. Sew a corner block onto each end of the strips. Press the seams toward the red square.

3. Sew these borders to the top and bottom of your quilt top. Press the seams to the outside.

Once you have finished your 12 blocks, you can choose this alternative sashing if you wish.

CUTTING INSTRUCTIONS

From the reserved dark fabric, cut
❋ 34 – 2" x WOF (width of the fabric) strips

From the reserved medium fabric, cut
❋ 20 – 2" x WOF strips

SEWING INSTRUCTIONS

1. Sew 2 dark 2" strips and 1 medium 2" strip into a strip set with the medium color in the center. Press the seams to the dark. Make 16. Sub cut into 31 – 18½" sashing strips. Reserve the remainder of the strip sets.

2. Sew 2 medium 2" strips and 1 dark 2" strip into a strip set with the dark color in the center. Make 2. Press the seams to the dark. Sub cut into 40 – 2" sections.

3. Cut the reserved strip sets from Step 1 into 20 – 2" sections.

4. With the sections you cut in steps 2 and 3 – make a 9-patch unit with the medium fabrics on the outside. Make 20. These units are the cornerstones.

5. Refer to the setting diagram and stitch the sashing sections, cornerstones and blocks together.

6. Layer, quilt and bind. Enjoy your quilt.

This Housewife Needle Case
was designed and stitched by
Glenn Dragone.

The housewife or *huswif* needle case was popular in the late-18th and early-19th centuries. Women fashioned them out of a variety of scrap fabrics and used them to store their precious needles and other sewing supplies, and kept them at hand for frequent use.

It is likely that a sewing kit or *huswif* would have been among the items carried with the participants traveling with the Corp of Discovery.

Housewife Needle Case

MATERIALS

* ¼ yard each of 5 fabrics of your choice
* 15" x 6" of lightweight cotton or cotton/poly batting
* Pinch of poly fiberfill or batting (for stuffed flower pincushion)
* Embroidery floss
* 10" square of freezer paper
* 1 small piece of thin leather cord or ribbon for button closure
* 1 button
* Basic sewing supplies

Housewife Needle Case

INSTRUCTIONS

1. Cut a 15" x 6" piece for the inside liner.

2. Cut 15¼" x 6" piece for the exterior shell. The ¼" of extra fabric allows for ease when it is sewn together.

3. Cut a 6½" square of each of the 5 fabrics for the pockets. Fold all 5 pocket pieces in half with the right sides together. Gently press the newly formed rectangle so there is a crease at the fold. Sew along the bottom edge using a ¼" seam allowance. Trim each pocket to measure 6" wide, press and turn inside out so the wrong sides are facing. The crease indicates the top of the pocket. Starting 4" from the top of the inside liner, position each rectangle, ensuring that the folded crease is exposed and at the top. A 1" overlap will allow all 5 to fit.

4. After all the pockets have been arranged, pin only the first one to the background. Remove the rest. Using a ¼" seam allowance, sew across the bottom of the first pinned pocket along the seamed edge.

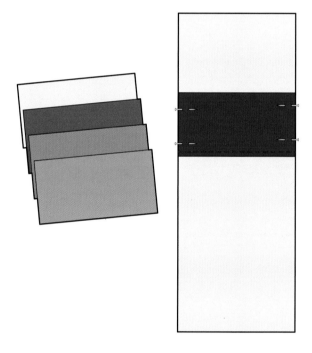

5. Pin the 2nd pocket in the rotation to the background piece. Keep in mind that it should lie on top of the first one and overlap by 1" on the bottom. Sew across the seamed edge of the pocket. Continue with the remaining pockets.

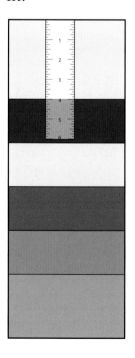

6. Trace the flower onto freezer paper. (You will find the pattern on page 64) Press the freezer paper onto the fabric. Cut out the flower adding a ⅛" seam allowance. Appliqué it onto the top 4" portion of the inside liner. Stuff the flower with a pinch of poly fill or batting before you get all the way around, then finish the appliqué process.

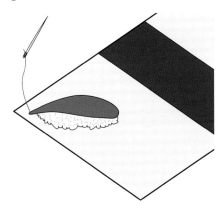

7. With a fabric-marking pencil and a light touch, draw the swirl stem and leaves. You can use a freehand method or use the pattern on page 64. Embroider the stem using either a stem stitch or split stitch. Embroider the outline of the leaves and finish by making French knots inside the leaves.

8. Cut a 15" x 6" piece of batting. Place the batting on the wrong side of the finished inside liner and sew around all 4 sides. This step simply tacks down all the pockets and keeps the batting in place.

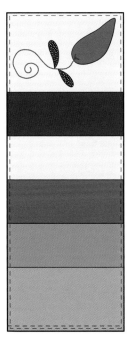

9. Mark with a pin where you would like the placement of the bird. Trace the bird onto freezer paper then appliqué in place. (You will find the pattern on page 65.) Using the fabric pencil, lightly mark the tail detail and embroider using a split stitch and French knots.

10. Cut binding strips 2" x 46" long. Press in half lengthwise, wrong sides together. Layer the inside liner and exterior shell, and sew binding to the outside edges. Leave an opening at the top middle to insert the button closure, finish sewing the binding in place. Blind stitch the binding on the other side.

11. Sew a button to the lower portion of the outside to fit inside the closure.

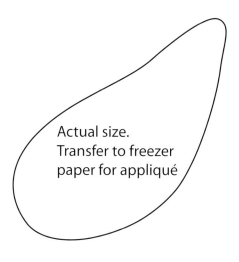

Actual size.
Transfer to freezer
paper for appliqué

Split stitch the entire outline starting just inside of the bottom of the stuffed pin cushion.

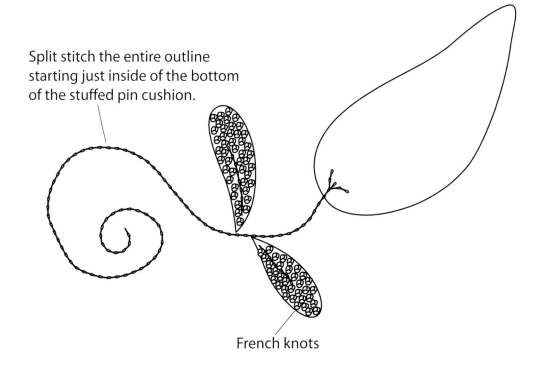

French knots

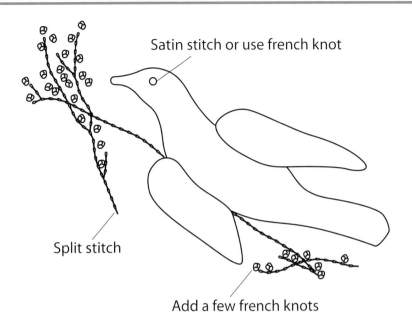

Satin stitch or use french knot

Split stitch

Add a few french knots

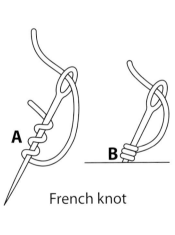

French knot

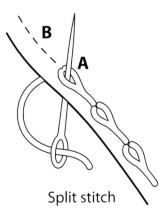

Split stitch

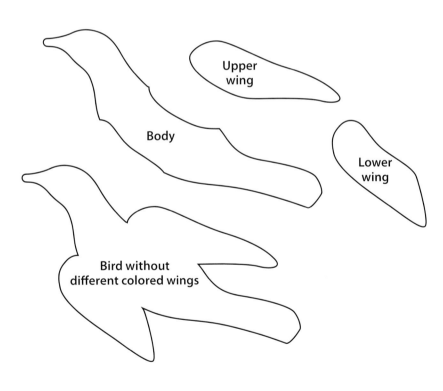

Upper wing

Body

Lower wing

Bird without different colored wings

Running Horse Needle Punch
designed by Laurie Simpson,
made by Logan O'Bier.

Running Horse Needle Punch

MATERIALS

FLOSS

* 3 skeins Buckeye Scarlet (Gentle Arts)
* 2 skeins Schoolhouse Red (Gentle Arts)
* 1 skein Claret (Gentle Arts)
* 1 skein Cranberry (Gentle Arts)
* 1 skein Midnight (Gentle Arts)
* 1 skein Freedom (Gentle Arts)
* 1 skein Wrought Iron (Gentle Arts)
* 1 skein Cornflower (Gentle Arts)
* 1 skein Dungarees (Gentle Arts)
* 1 skein Blue Jay (Gentle Arts)
* 1 skein Antique Lace (Gentle Arts)
* 2 skeins Honey Dew (Gentle Arts)
* 2 skeins Shaker White (Gentle Arts)
* 2 skeins Oatmeal (Gentle Arts)
* 1 skein Parchment (Gentle Arts)
* 1 skein Cayenne (Week's Dye Works)

NEEDLE PUNCH TOOLS

* Needle Punch Threader
* Hoop

OTHER SUPPLIES

* 10" x 12" piece of weaver's cloth
* Frame Top Box
* Fine-tip permanent marker – Sharpie or Micron Pigma pen
* Scissors
* Lightweight Cardboard

Running Horse Needle Punch

INSTRUCTIONS

1. Trace the horse design onto the weaver's cloth with a permanent, fine-tip marker. (Remember, you work from the back when you needle punch. Your design is a reverse image of what you want. So... if you want your horse facing right — you need to draw him facing left on your weaver's cloth.)

2. Refer to the photo for color placement. The varying degrees and shades listed will give your project depth and texture. Use the blues for the horse, the lights for the background and the reds in the border.

3. Punch in the design using three strands of floss. Begin with the outline of the shape on which you are working. Fill in that area, staying within the lines. Trim the thread ends flush with the tufts of thread.

4. Once the design is filled in, stretch it over a cardboard sheet and tape the raw ends to the back. Center it into a frame top box.

Salmonberries Penny Rug was
designed by Laurie Simpson and
stitched by Debbie Duckworth.
Finished size: 23" x 18".

Salmonberries Penny Rug

MATERIALS

※ 18" x 24" rectangle of light wool for background and
tongues – Cut an 18" square and reserve the remainder
for the tongues

※ 19" square of cotton fabric for backing

※ 12" square of blue/green wool for stems
and berry caps

※ 12" x 7" rectangle of green/brown wool for vase

※ Assorted blue wools – enough to equal
a 12" square for leaves

※ Assorted red wools – enough to equal
a 10" square for berries and bird

※ Pearl Cotton – 1 skein each
of gold, dark blue, neutral
and red

※ Basic sewing supplies

※ Long reach stapler
(optional)

※ Freezer paper

Salmonberries Penny Rug

INSTRUCTIONS

1. Following the Salmonberries quilt block diagram and templates (pages 45, 99 – 100), draw the template shapes and edge tongues onto freezer paper. Iron the templates onto the appropriate color of wool.

2. Cut out the shapes **without** adding a seam allowance. Staple or pin the basket to the background fabric and stitch in place using a blanket stitch and the pearl cotton. Place each shape onto the background wool and stitch with the pearl cotton using a blanket stitch, except for the berry caps - which will be sewn on last and attached with a straight stitch and French knots.

3. Stitch the berry seeds with the gold pearl cotton using the French knot stitch.

4. Blanket stitch, using the neutral pearl cotton, around each of the tongues. Do not stitch the area that will be tucked under the background.

5. Staple or pin the tongues onto the top and bottom of the background wool. Stitch around the outside edge using a blanket stitch and the neutral pearl cotton. As you stitch, you will be stitching the ends of the tongues in place.

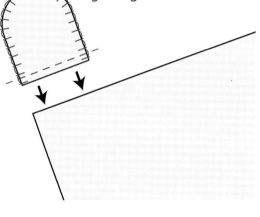

Staple or pin the blanket-stitched tongue to the underside of the penny rug using a 1/4" seam allowance.

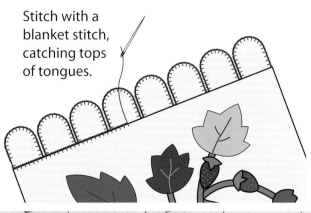

Stitch with a blanket stitch, catching tops of tongues.

6. Center the backing fabric onto the back of the penny rug. Turn the raw edges under and stitch with a blind hem stitch. Enjoy your Penny Rug.

Tongue
Cut 16

Scrap Rug designed and hooked by Polly Minick. This is Polly's adaption of a mid-1800s rug. Finished size: Approximately 22" x 43".

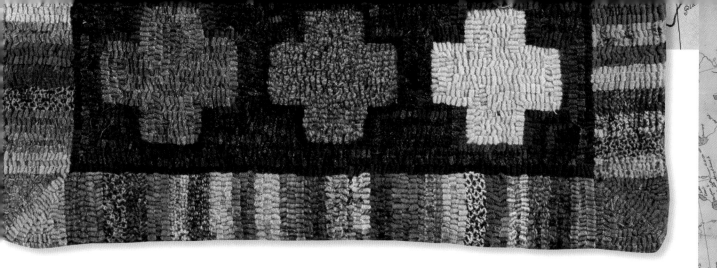

This rug was designed to use leftover strips and scraps that remain after each project you complete. At the turn of the century, it was very important not to be wasteful and people of that era were champions when it came to "using up and making do."

Scrap Rug

MATERIALS

WOOL

❋ ½ yard total of a mix of 6 different antique blacks – mix in different textures as well

❋ 21 – ⅛ yard each of a mix of colors to use in the crosses and the border

❋ 12 additional coordinating colors (enough to equal ¾ yard) for the border

ADDITIONAL SUPPLIES

❋ 1 yard linen or Monk's Cloth

❋ 1 yard backing for your rug

❋ Hoop or frame

❋ Rug Hooking Hook

❋ Red Dot Tracing Material

❋ Black Magic Marker

❋ Scissors

❋ 4 yards tape for binding. The width of the binding should be anywhere from 2" – 3½".

Scrap Rug

INSTRUCTIONS

1. This is an easy rug to hook and you will love using up your wonderful "leftovers!"

2. Enlarge the pattern on opposite page to 476 percent at your favorite copy shop.

3. Trace the enlarged pattern onto the Red Dot tracing material. Place the Red Dot tracing on top of the linen and retrace it using the black magic marker. This will transfer your pattern to the linen.

4. Begin by hooking all the crosses and use many colors but make sure they work together. You don't want any of the colors to clash or stand out from the others.

5. I sew on the binding tape before I start hooking. By using this technique, one can hook right up to the tape and get a nice even edge. After all the crosses are completed, it is time to work on the background.

6. Use the mix of antique blacks for the background. Cut enough strips, using a #8 blade to fill a basket and pick them out randomly. This will give the rug an aged look as well as movement and texture.

7. Don't cut all the wool at one time; it makes it harder to measure what you need to finish. To know how much you need to complete an image – fold the piece of wool five times and lay on the area in question. If it covers the image, you will have enough.

8. After you have completed filling in the background, you are ready to hook the random striped border. Use as many of the colors that were used to the make the crosses as possible and add in the coordinating colors as you hook.

9. When doing a border like this you do **not** have to draw the lines for the stripes. You can easily make it up as you go. Your strips should all be cut about the same size.

10. Start at a corner and work towards the center. Since the stripes are random, you can sometimes use one hooked row but you will want to use two hooked rows for the most part. Occasionally hook three rows.

11. After you have worked about one-half of the way across, stop and go to the other corner and begin again, working towards the center. If you are one hooked row off, it will be easier to conceal the extra row in the middle of the border than at the corner.

12. When you have finished hooking, steam the rug, trim off the excess linen, turn the binding tape over and hand stitch the edge to complete your project.

13. Always sign your rug. Some hookers hook their initials into the rug, some use a certain symbol, and many sign on the back.

Enlarge 476%

MATERIALS

* 1⅛ yards of a mixture of antique black wool for the background
* ¼ yard medium blue for basket and flowers
* ½ yard (mixed textures) gold for border stripe and flower centers
* 1/16 yard gold/black tweed for basket
* ⅛ yard terra cotta or bittersweet wool for flowers
* ⅛ yard old red for flowers
* ¾ yard total mixture of olive greens for stems and leaves

This rug is my interpretation of a mid-1800s rug that was owned by friends of mine. I thought the undersized basket and all the flowers and leaves were stunning. I redesigned it and took a few liberties with the basket of flowers. The original also had a multitude of borders, many of which I omitted.

Antique Basket of Flowers Rug

Antique Basket of Flowers rug designed and hooked by Polly Minick. Finished size: 28" x 44".

ADDITIONAL SUPPLIES
* 1⅛ yards Linen or Monk's Cloth
* 1⅛ yards backing fabric
* Hoop or frame
* Rug Hooking Hook
* Red Dot Tracing Material
* Black Magic Marker
* Scissors
* 4¼ yards tape for binding. The width of the binding should be anywhere from 2" – 3½".

Antique Basket of Flowers Rug

INSTRUCTIONS

1. Enlarge the pattern below to 588 percent at your favorite copy shop.

2. Trace the enlarged pattern onto the Red Dot tracing material. Place the Red Dot tracing on top of the linen and retrace it using the black magic marker. This will transfer your pattern to the linen.

3. I sew on the binding tape before I start hooking. By using this technique, one can hook right up to the tape.

4. Hook the basket first, then the leaves and stems. Feel free to choose different colors of wools for the flowers, as we know they can be any color one desires.

5. After hooking the flowers, leaves and stems, begin filling in the background. It's important to use many shades of antique black because it gives the rug texture, movement and makes it look old.

6. When you have finished hooking, steam the rug, trim off the excess linen, turn the binding tape over and hand stitch the edge to complete your project.

7. Always sign your rug. Some hookers hook their initials into the rug, some use a certain symbol and many sign on the back.

Enlarge 588%

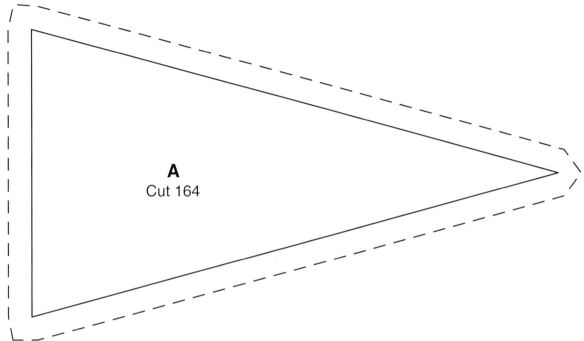

A
Cut 164

Border Templates

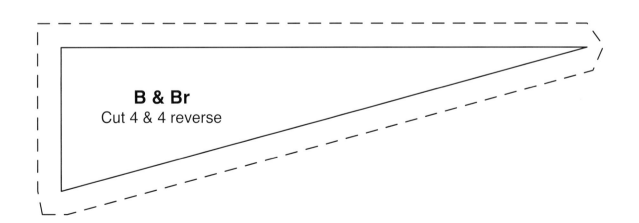

B & Br
Cut 4 & 4 reverse

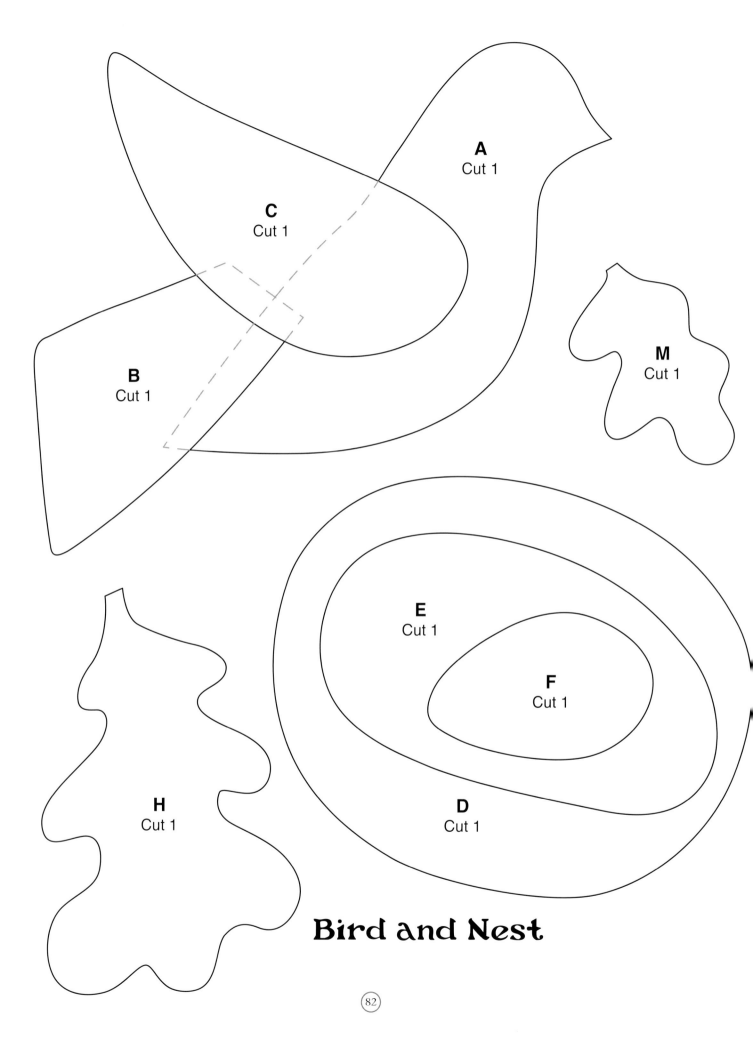

A
Cut 1

C
Cut 1

B
Cut 1

M
Cut 1

E
Cut 1

F
Cut 1

D
Cut 1

H
Cut 1

Bird and Nest

Bird and Nest

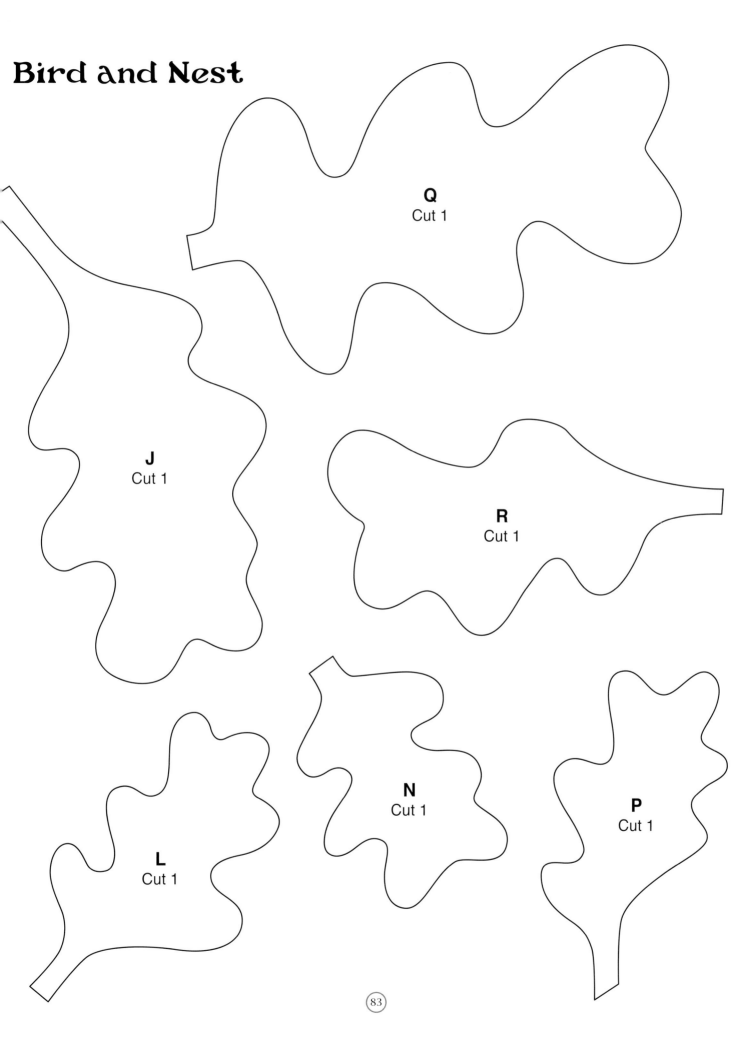

Q
Cut 1

J
Cut 1

R
Cut 1

N
Cut 1

L
Cut 1

P
Cut 1

K
Cut 1

I
Cut 1

O
Cut 1

Bird and Nest

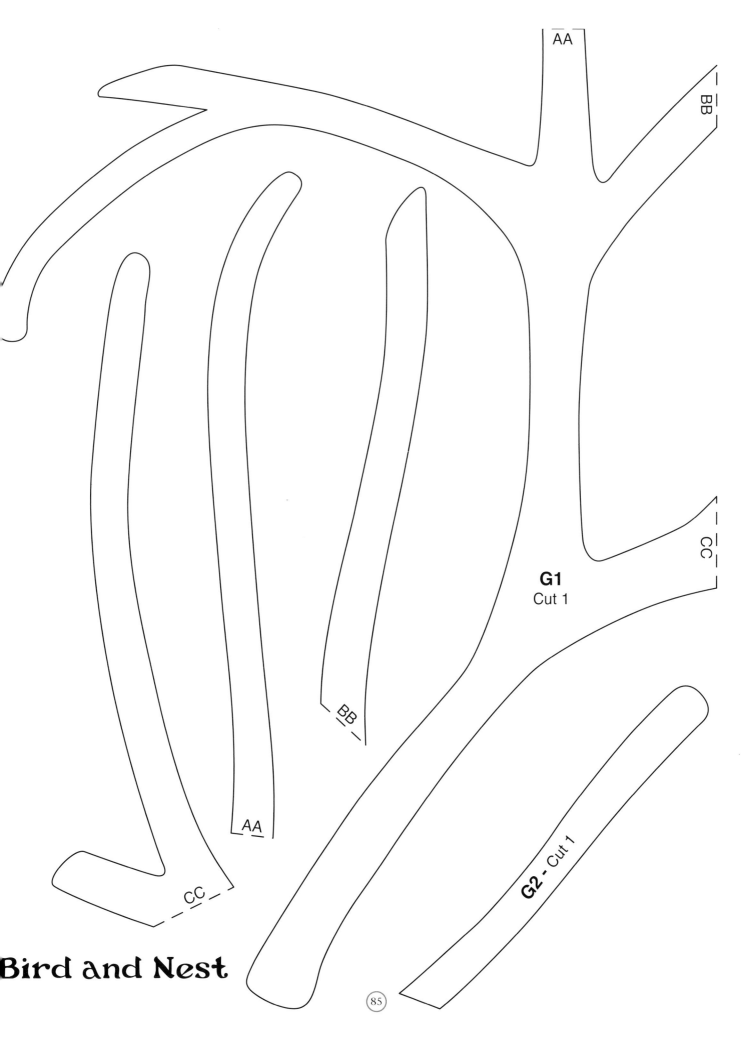

AA

BB

CC

G1
Cut 1

BB

AA

CC

G2 - Cut 1

Bird and Nest

Mariner's Compass

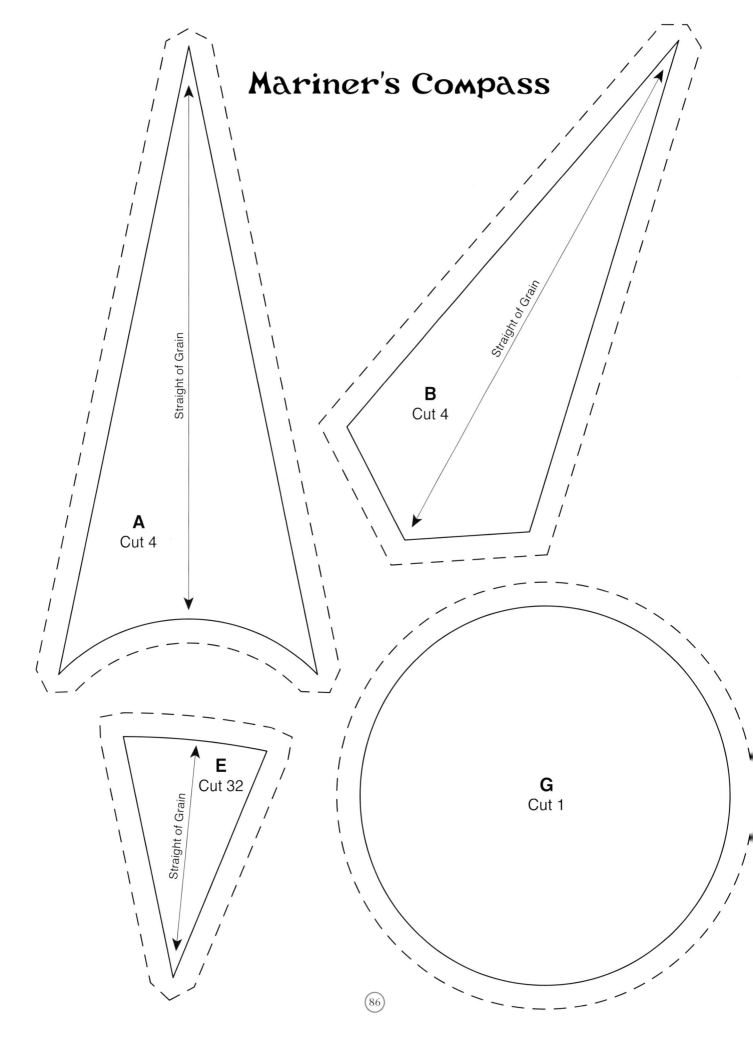

A
Cut 4

Straight of Grain

B
Cut 4

Straight of Grain

E
Cut 32

Straight of Grain

G
Cut 1

Mariner's Compass

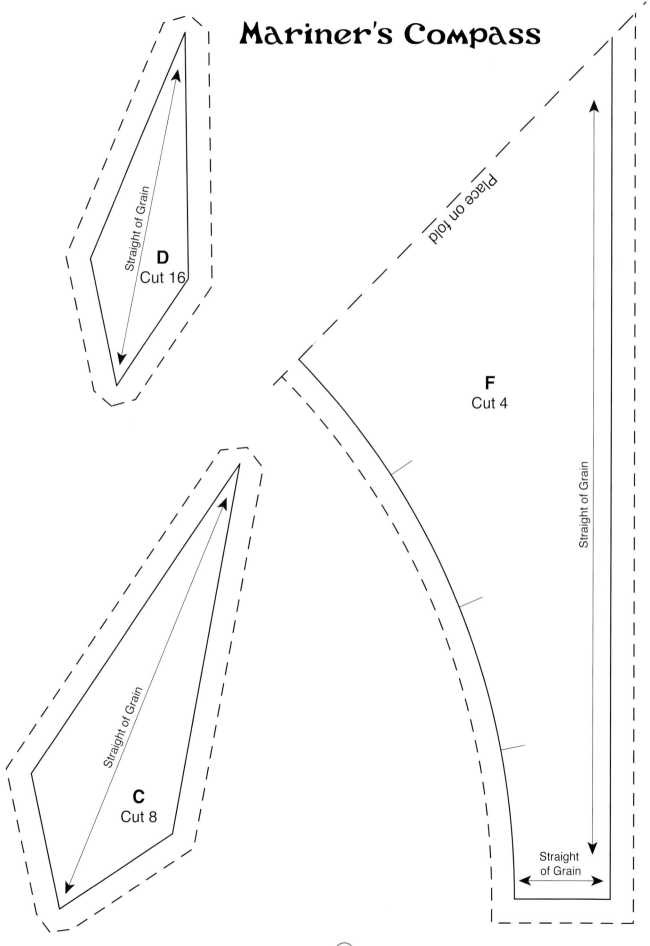

D
Cut 16

Straight of Grain

C
Cut 8

Straight of Grain

Place on fold

F
Cut 4

Straight of Grain

Straight of Grain

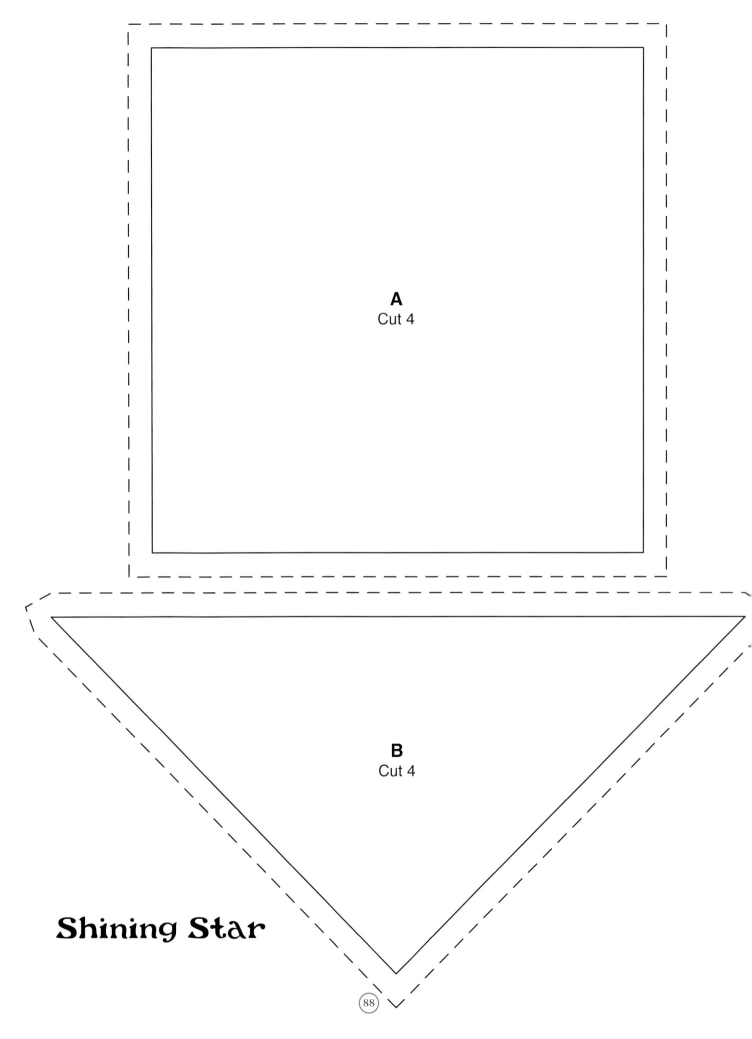

A
Cut 4

B
Cut 4

Shining Star

88

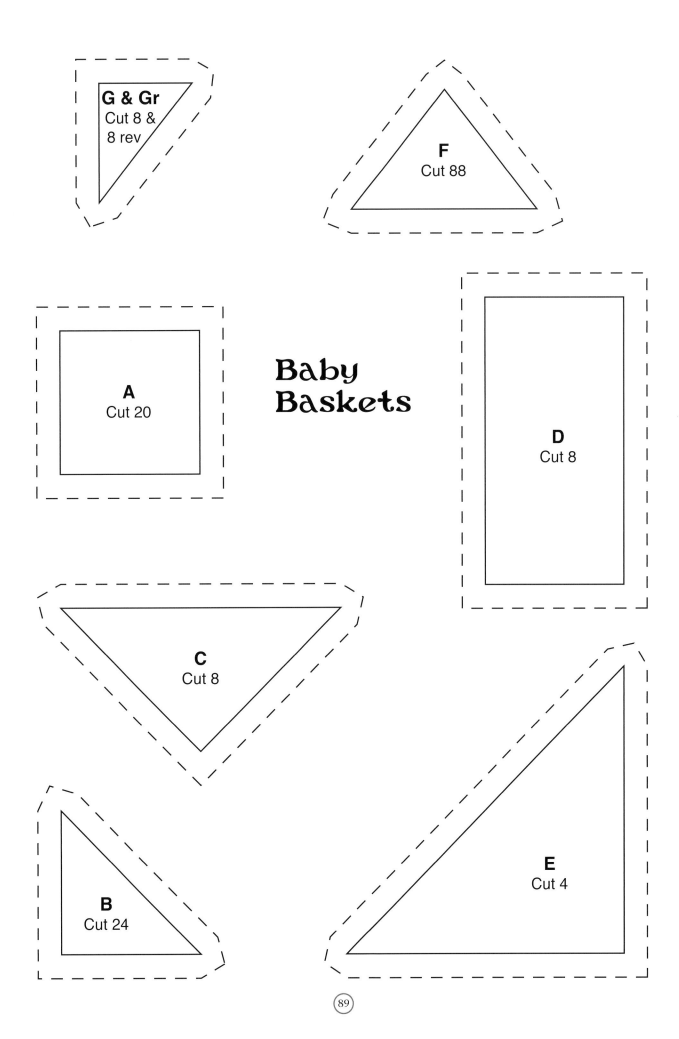

G & Gr
Cut 8 &
8 rev

F
Cut 88

A
Cut 20

Baby
Baskets

D
Cut 8

C
Cut 8

E
Cut 4

B
Cut 24

Crossed Canoes

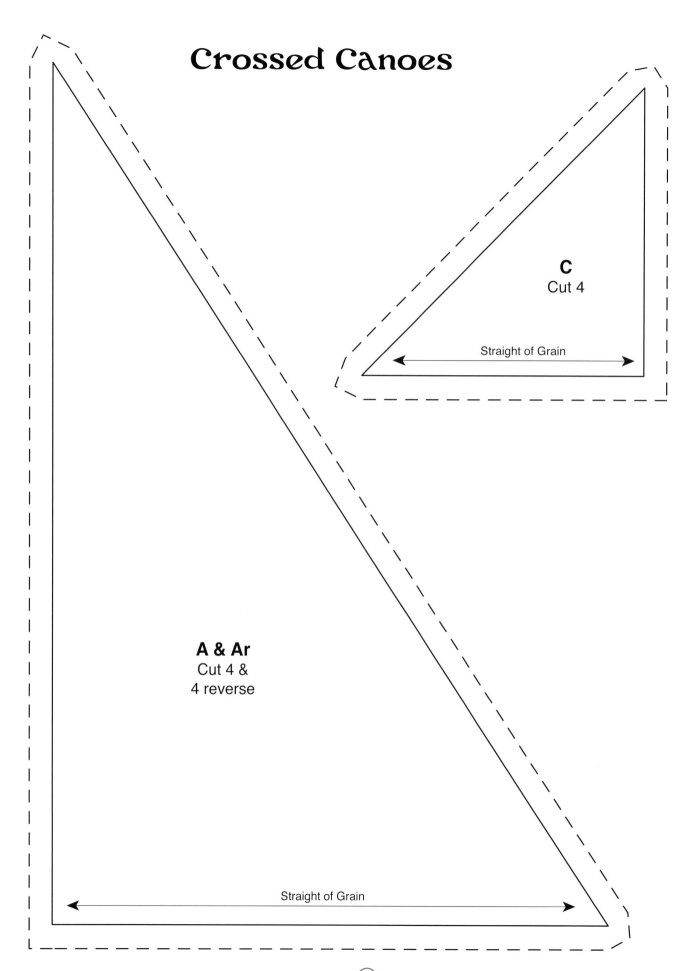

C
Cut 4

Straight of Grain

A & Ar
Cut 4 &
4 reverse

Straight of Grain

Crossed Canoes

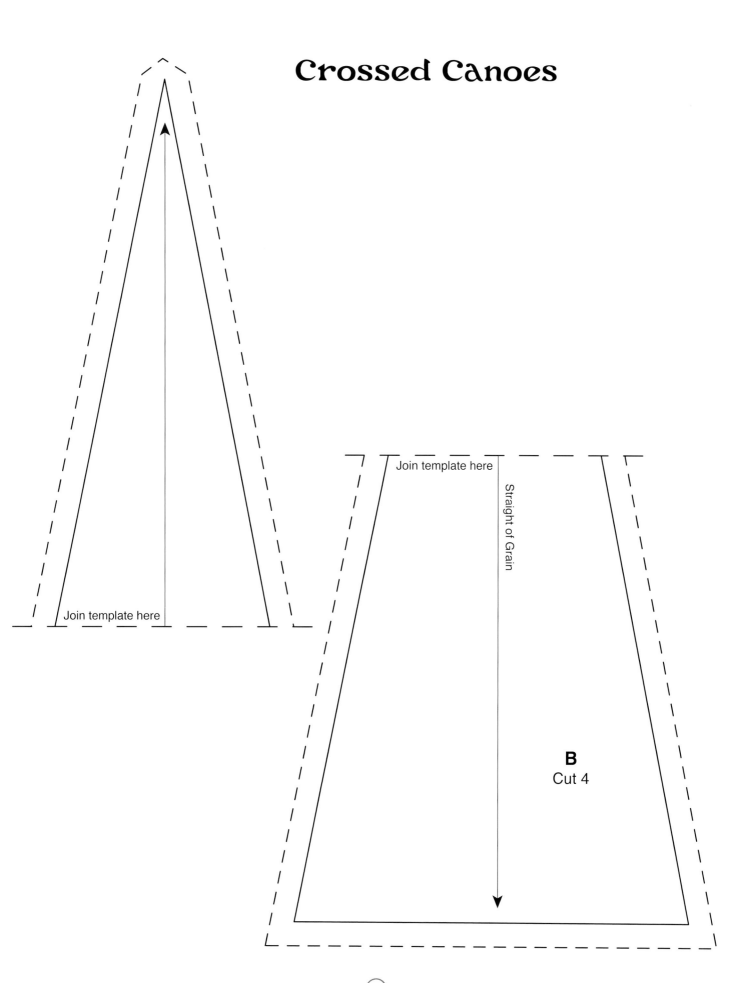

Join template here

Join template here

Straight of Grain

B
Cut 4

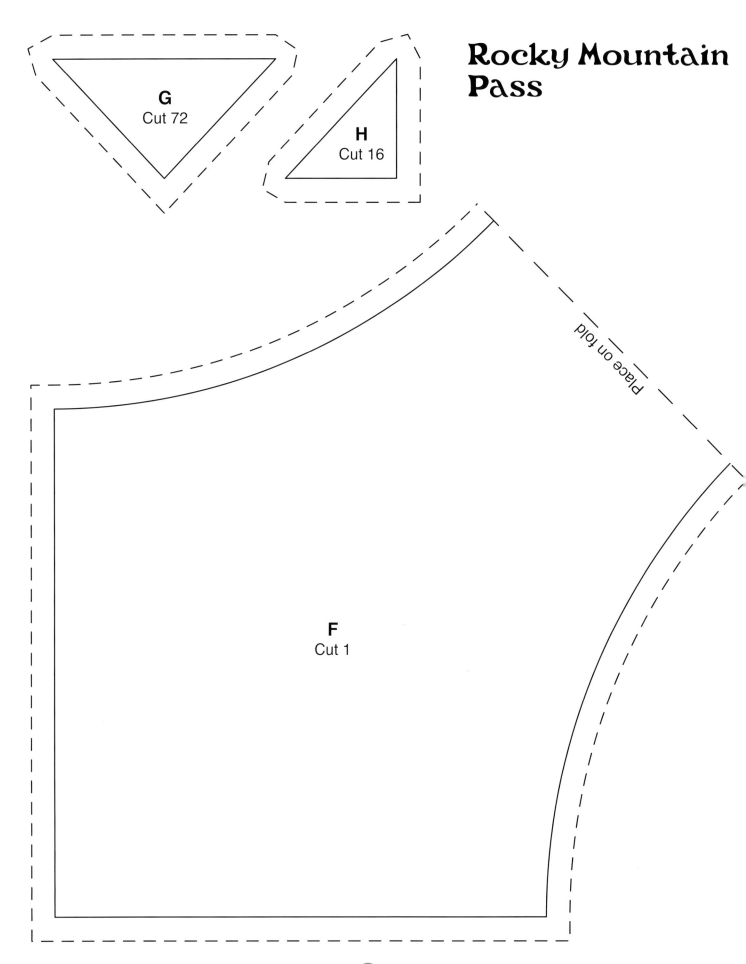

Rocky Mountain Pass

G
Cut 72

H
Cut 16

F
Cut 1

Place on fold

Rocky Mountain Pass

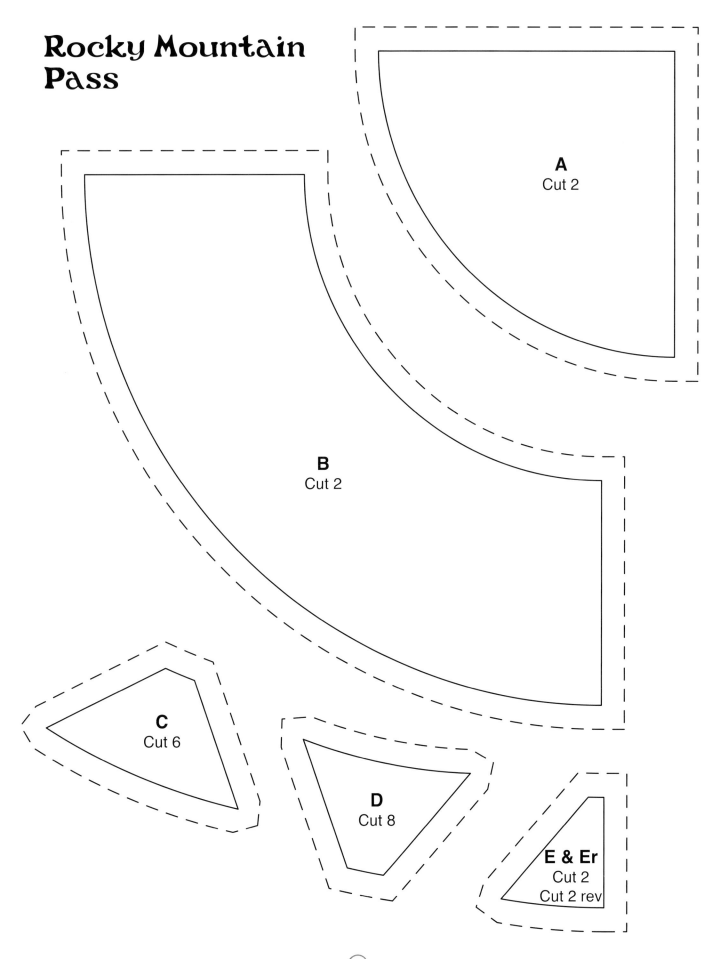

A
Cut 2

B
Cut 2

C
Cut 6

D
Cut 8

E & Er
Cut 2
Cut 2 rev

Horses

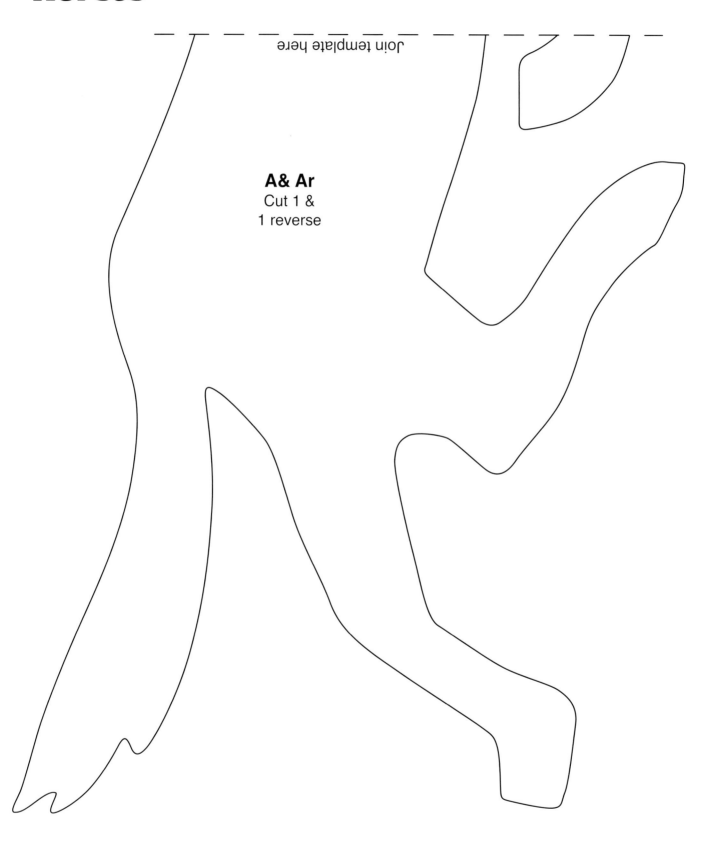

Join template here

A& Ar
Cut 1 &
1 reverse

Horses

Join template here

Deer Fern

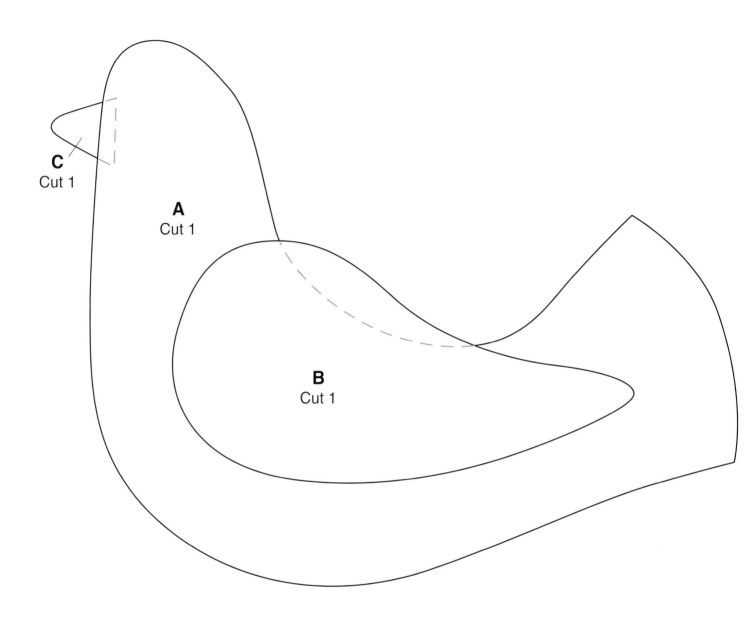

C
Cut 1

A
Cut 1

B
Cut 1

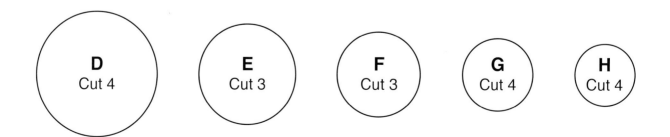

D
Cut 4

E
Cut 3

F
Cut 3

G
Cut 4

H
Cut 4

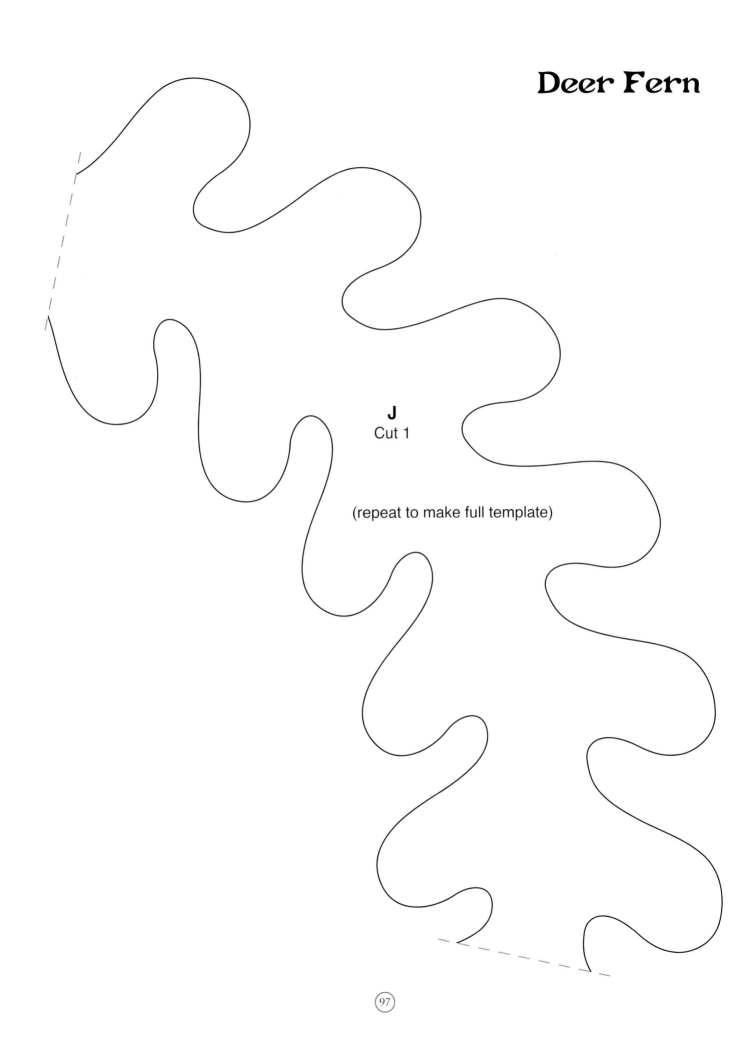

Deer Fern

J
Cut 1

(repeat to make full template)

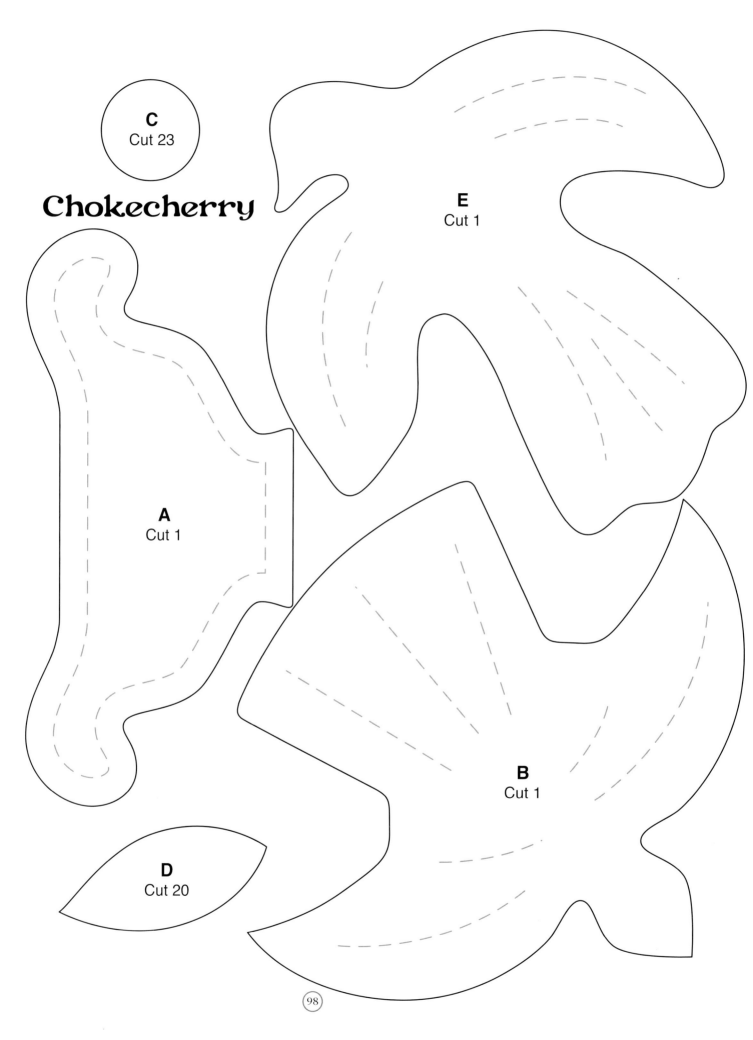

C
Cut 23

Chokecherry

E
Cut 1

A
Cut 1

B
Cut 1

D
Cut 20

98

Salmonberry

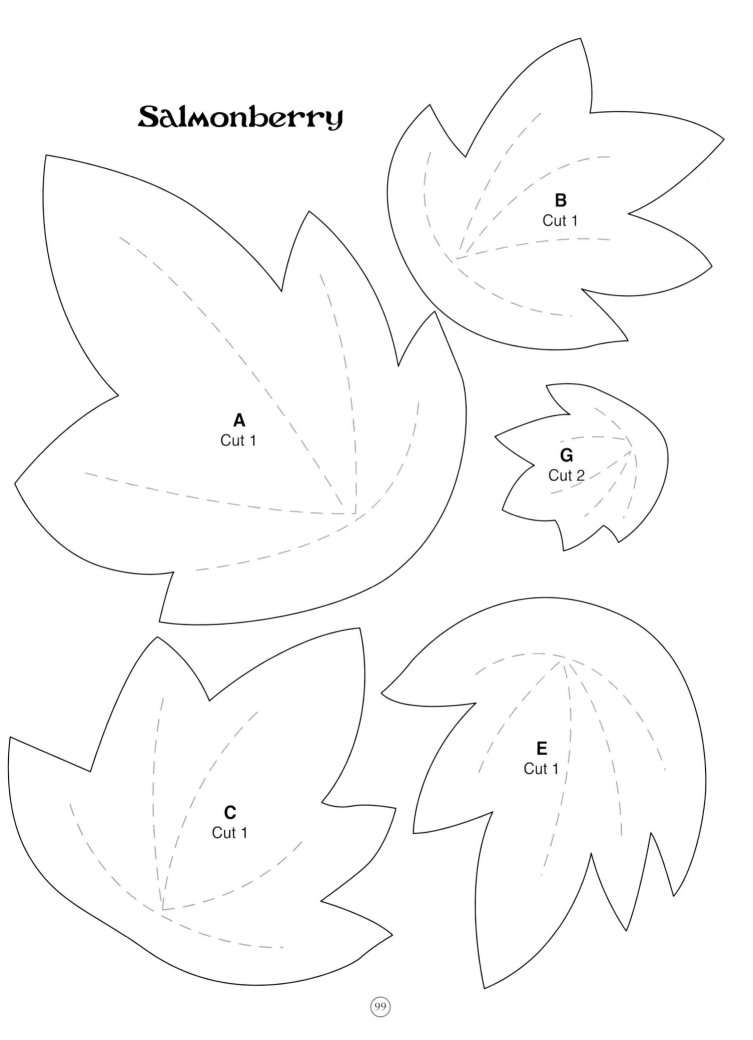

B
Cut 1

A
Cut 1

G
Cut 2

C
Cut 1

E
Cut 1

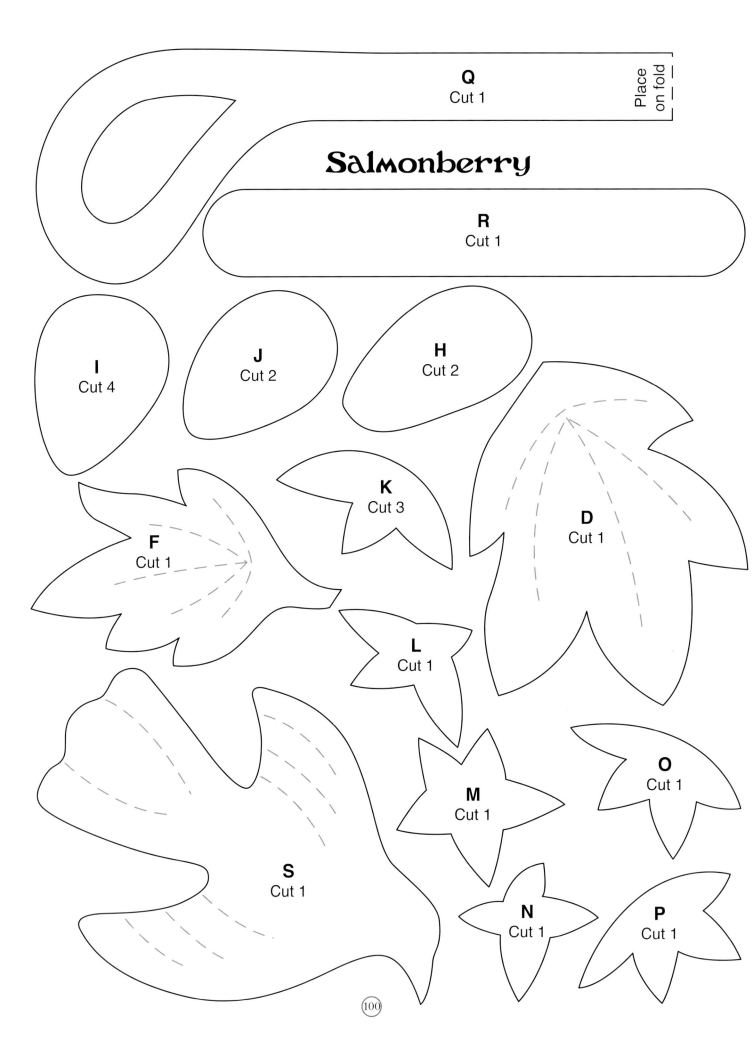

Q
Cut 1

Place on fold

Salmonberry

R
Cut 1

I
Cut 4

J
Cut 2

H
Cut 2

D
Cut 1

K
Cut 3

F
Cut 1

L
Cut 1

O
Cut 1

M
Cut 1

S
Cut 1

N
Cut 1

P
Cut 1

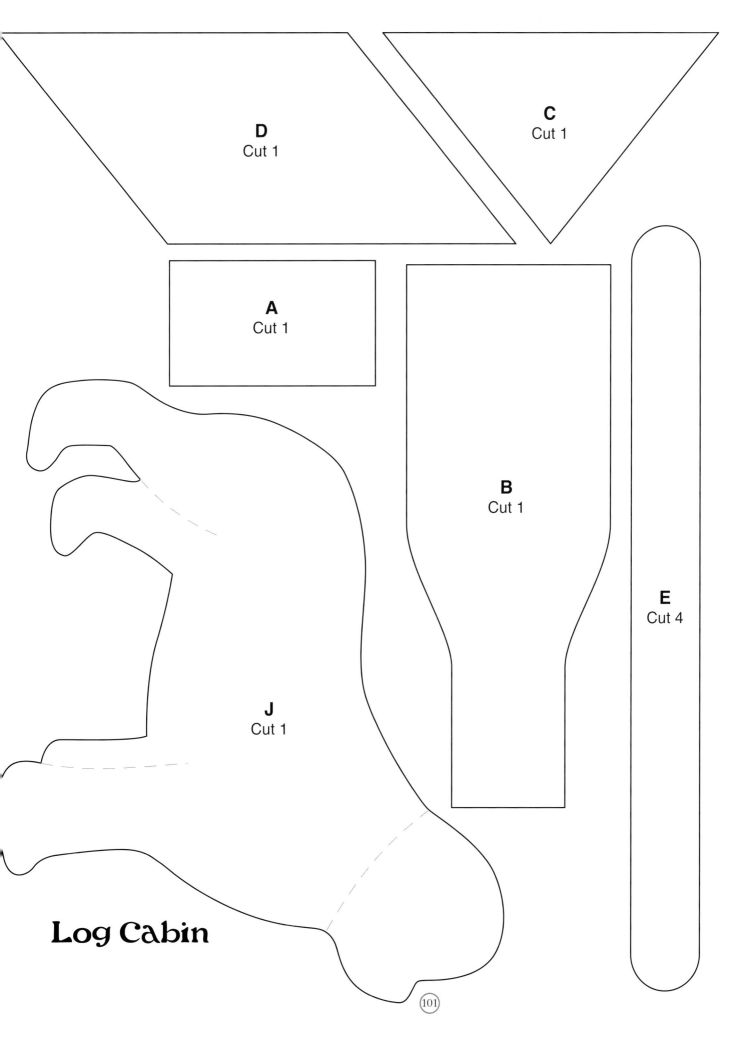

D
Cut 1

C
Cut 1

A
Cut 1

B
Cut 1

E
Cut 4

J
Cut 1

Log Cabin

101

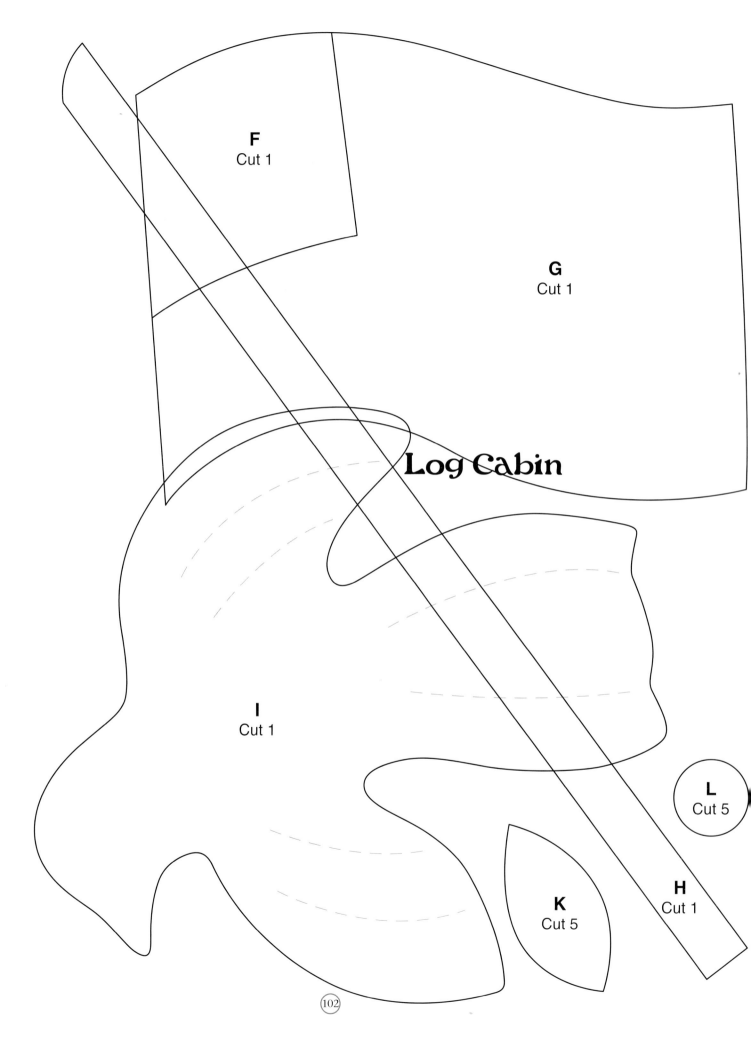

F
Cut 1

G
Cut 1

Log Cabin

I
Cut 1

L
Cut 5

K
Cut 5

H
Cut 1